Physical Characteristics of the Shetland Sheepdog

(from The Kennel Club breed standard)

SIZE
Ideal height at withers: dogs 37 cms (14.5 ins); bitches 35.5 e than 2.5 cms (one inch) above or below ghly undesirable.

COLOUR
Sable, clear or shaded; tricolour with intense black on body, rich tan markings preferred; blue merle; black and white and black and tan.

TAIL
Set low; tapering bone reaches to at least hock; with abundant hair and slightly upward sweep. May be slightly raised when moving but never over level of back. Never kinked.

HINDQUARTERS
Thigh broad and muscular, thigh bones set into pelvis at right angles. Stifle joint has distinctive angle, hock joint clean cut, angular, well let down with strong bone. Hocks straight when viewed from behind.

FEET
Oval soles, well padded, toes arched and close together.

Shetland Sheepdog

$\diamond$

by Charlotte Schwartz

Table of Contents

History of the Shetland Sheepdog

Trace the beginnings of the Shetland Sheepdog as a skilled sheep-herder in the rugged Scottish mountain country and follow its spread in popularity around the world as a companion dog, show dog, competition dog and ambassador of canine good will.

Personality of the Shetland Sheepdog

Friendly, outgoing and intelligent, the Shetland Sheepdog is both a hard worker and a wonderful choice for a companion dog. Find out about the personality and physical characteristics of the Sheltie, as well as breed-specific health concerns.

Breed Standard for the Shetland Sheepdog

Learn the requirements of a well-bred Shetland Sheepdog by studying the description of the breed set forth in The Kennel Club standard. Both show dogs and pets must possess key characteristics as outlined in the breed standard.

Your Puppy Shetland Sheepdog

Be advised about choosing a reputable breeder and selecting a healthy, typical puppy. Understand the responsibilities of ownership, including home preparation, acclimatization, the vet and prevention of common puppy problems.

PUBLISHED IN THE
UNITED KINGDOM BY:

INTERPET
P U B L I S H I N G

Vincent Lane, Dorking
Surrey RH4 3YX
England

ISBN 1-902389-31-X

Everyday Care of Your Shetland Sheepdog

Enter into a sensible discussion of dietary and feeding considerations, exercise, grooming, travelling and identification of your dog. This chapter discusses Shetland Sheepdog care for all stages of development.

Photo Credits:

Photos by Carol Ann Johnson, with additional photos by:

Norvia Behling
Carolina Biological Supply
Doskocil
Isabelle Francais
James Hayden-Yoav
James R. Hayden, RBP
Bill Jonas
Dwight R. Kuhn

Dr Dennis Kunkel
Mikki Pet Products
Phototake
Jean Claude Revy
Charlotte Schwartz
Dr Andrew Spielman
Karen Taylor
C. James Webb

Special thanks to Caudine Altier, Agnes Fallèri, Muriel Jochem, Nancy Runyon, Emeric L'Esterazur du Lac and all owners of dogs featured in this book.
Illustrations by Renée Low

History of the
SHETLAND SHEEPDOG

Stand atop a hillside overlooking an emerald valley. Feel the soft summer breeze rising up from the land below to bring you the scent of green grass and lush vegetation. Scan the valley that runs for several miles beneath you. Notice the beige cloud that slowly undulates across the valley, then look again.

It's not a cloud. It's a flock of hundreds of sheep moving as one across the field. Wonder now at what keeps them together and forces them to move in such beautiful symmetry. Focus on the sheep cloud as your eyes adjust to the scene. Only then will you notice two small dark creatures around the outside of the flock.

Those dark specks are Shetland Sheepdogs, developed for use in the Shetland Islands off the northern coast of Scotland. The dogs are doing what they've been doing for hundreds of years: keeping the flock together and guiding the path of its travel. They are herding sheep.

They take directions from a distant herdsman who whistles his orders to them. The sound of his whistling starts and stops the dogs, turns them backwards and forwards, right and left. He often directs them to go fetch a stray ewe as it wanders away from the flock.

As you watch the dogs work, marvel at the wonder of these small creatures handling hundreds of sheep, each of which weighs many times more than a Shetland Sheepdog.

Now wonder no more: Here within these pages is the story of how and why these little dogs manage such great feats. Their story truly is remarkable considering that they are descended from the great strong collies of ancient Scotland.

This whole Shetland thing began thousands of years ago in the rugged mountain country of Scotland known as the Highlands. It is their skill and intelligence at handling animals such as sheep, cattle and reindeer that fostered their development and has sustained them as unsurpassed herders even into the 21st century.

Opposite page: Aside from being a magnificent, beautiful representative of the dog world, the Shetland Sheepdog is a warm, loving pet for millions of homes around the world.

The Shetland Sheepdog, though originally bred for herding sheep, has also shown great skills and aptitude in herding cattle.

Lacking authentic historical records regarding the origin of Shetland Sheepdogs, we are left to take bits and pieces of information—stories, occasional written references, paintings, old tales passed from one generation to the next—to recreate a most probable scenario for the breed's beginning. Thus goes the story.

As far back as Neolithic times, 3500 to 2000 BC, there were collie-type northern sheepdogs that were finding their way south into the Mediterranean countries. From there they eventually travelled with merchant traders to the British Isles.

Going back even further, we find that these collie-type dogs descended from northern Euro-pean and Asian wolves, thus making the dogs genetically pre-disposed to herding and manip-ulating large flocks of animals. Wolves obtain food by using this method of rounding up their prey in order to pick out a can-didate for the kill. The collie-type dogs of today therefore still carry within their genes the traits for herding.

In addition, modern collie-type dogs rely on a master, a human, to oversee their work. This trait comes from the origi-nal wolves that needed an alpha wolf to guide them in the roundup and the hunt. Absent a leader, neither the wolves of ancient times nor the dogs of today would survive and prosper. Both are social animals.

About the time that the collie-type dogs were settling in England and Scotland, the farmers of the Shetland Islands, known as crofters, were using dogs to herd their flocks of sheep. They paid little attention to the size and uniformity of the dogs—they were concerned only with the dogs' ability to work.

However, when they visited the mountainous Highlands of Scotland, they became fascinated with the large collies of the mainland. The intelligence and dedication of those big dogs were qualities much desired in working dogs, and the Shetland Islanders began using them to improve and refine their own 'toonies' or local 'township' dogs.

Scottish, Dutch and Scandinavian fishermen also stopped at the Shetland Islands with some frequency. Occasionally they brought with them dogs they kept on board their vessels. On one occasion, as an old yarn tells us, a yacht touched the island and on board was a black-and-tan King Charles Spaniel. This dog eventually bred with some of the island dogs, thus launching the true beginning of the Shetland Sheepdogs.

Their size was the only problem. Shetland sheep are about one-half the size of the

The black and tan King Charles Spaniel has been associated in folk legend with having been introduced into the bloodlines of the Shetland Sheepdog.

black-faced sheep of Scotland. The Islanders realised from the beginning that they needed smaller collie-type dogs than those found in the Highlands. Thus they chose the smallest Scottish dogs to breed to their own toonies. Eventually, they produced very small collie-type dogs that they named Shetland Sheepdogs.

The end result produced a dog of distinction.

Did You Know?

'Lord Scott' was the first Sheltie registered with the American Kennel Club in 1911. 'Sheltieland Alice Grey Gown' was the one-millionth Sheltie registered in 1935.

The Sheltie, as it became known, closely resembled a large collie in appearance with the happy disposition and friendly characteristics of the spaniel and the heart, stamina and dedication to master of the English collie.

Even later dogs were cross-bred with native dogs of Greenland known as Yaks. Traces of these crosses are seen today in the large erect ears and heavy coat of the Sheltie. It seems safe to say that today's Sheltie is a combination of old native island dogs; large northern collies; spaniels; and Yaks from the frigid climate of Greenland.

The earliest record of the true Shetland Sheepdog dates back to 1840 in the form of an engraving of the town of Lerwick, capital of the Shetland Islands. It shows a Shetland pony in the background and a small collie-type dog in the foreground.

Then, in 1944, a traveller to the Shetland Islands wrote an article about the local sheepdogs that herded the flocks by day, then played and slept in the house of the herdsman by night.

As time passed, the crofters began managing larger flocks that in turn required larger collie-type dogs. Collies from the mainland were again introduced to increase the size of the Shetland dogs, and it was at this time that Shetland farmers recognised the need to stabilise the size and appearance of the dogs, thus safeguarding the breeding of the Shetland Sheepdog for all time.

The dogs possessed great intelligence and stamina with fine muscular development and thick coats due to the harshness of their island environment.

Even though small in size, when compared to a Collie or another larger herding breed, the Shetland Sheepdog still can handle very large animals in its herding mode.

The Rough Collie is recognised in three colours, including sable, tricolour and the blue merle, shown here. The close relationship between Collies and Shelties is evident from the sharing of these three colour varieties.

These traits were carefully retained whilst size was added to bring the dogs to the size of 15 inches or 16 inches at the shoulder.

As the breed became stable and people could accurately predict the appearance and size of the Sheltie puppies, they began to be exhibited at local shows in and around Lerwick.

In 1906 the breed was shown for the first time at Crufts Dog Show in London, where the dog-show community enthusiastically received them. Then, in 1908, the Shetland Collie Club was founded. It wasn't until 1910 that Crufts offered separate classification for the breed for

Did You Know?

In 1472 the Shetland Islands became officially annexed to the Scottish Crown, giving the islanders a solid connection with the mainland. Following annexation, the islanders increased their travel between their island and Scotland to a point where they began comparing farming techniques and dog raising with their own methods.

13

The Shetland Sheepdog was introduced at the London Crufts Dog Show in 1906. It became an instant success and has been amongst the popular breeds in the UK ever since.

Did You Know?

World War I was almost the downfall of the Shetland Sheepdog. Breeding was almost completely halted and size and type were nearly lost. One breeder, however, introduced a collie crossbred into a limited breeding programme, thereby preserving the uniform type of well-bone sturdiness and size into his line. This act set the uniformity for future generations despite four years of war.

the first time. Both Scottish and English exhibitors provided a large entry that the public immediately embraced.

Shortly after that, the Ladies Kennel Association established classes for the dogs and their popularity exploded with entries equal to that of the regular Collies.

In 1911 the breed crossed the Atlantic and appeared at American shows with equal enthusiasm. However, the subject matter of size and type still plagued the breed in America.

In 1914 the English Sheepdog Club was formed and urged the adoption of a standard for the breed that included, 'the general appearance of the Shetland Collie as approximately that of a show Collie in miniature, ideal height at the shoulder, 12 inches.'

Later that same year The Kennel Club joined the Scottish and English Shetland Clubs to grant the breed individual classification. Now the Shetland Sheepdog was recognised as a breed on its own, not just as a miniature Collie.

Though controversy over size continued for several decades, the matter was finally put to rest in 1929 in America. At the famous Westminster Kennel Club Dog Show, the American Shetland Sheepdog Association united with the English and Scottish clubs to describe the breed as 'resembling a Collie (Rough) in miniature' with size being designated as 12 to 15 inches at the shoulder, the ideal being 13.5 inches. Eventually, the American Shetland Sheepdog Association changed their standard to read 'between 13 and 16 inches' with disqualification of any height above or below that range.

The difference of an inch or two in the size of the Shetland

Erect ears that tip forward are a hallmark that is shared between the Shetland Sheepdog and the Collie. In general appearance and colour as well as expression and head, the two breeds are remarkably similar.

Sheepdog is certainly secondary to its fundamental character. Moulded by the rugged land from which it came, the dog is a hard worker despite the rigours of the island's climate. His traits of intelligence, agility, soundness and dedication come from his relative, the large Collie. His love of master and family, his instinct to guard and protect, his

Did You Know?

The Shetland Islands are not just known for miniature collies. They are also known for other diminutive animals such as cattle, sheep and ponies.

15

Shetland Sheepdog

The Smooth Collie is one of the Shetland Sheepdog's close relatives. Of the two Collies, the Smooth is much less popular than the Rough. Shelties cannot be smooth-coated.

sweetness of disposition together with his fondness of the outdoors come from his spaniel and herding progenitors. These traits remain true and obvious even today and are what make the Sheltie a dog of distinction.

Proof of the continuity of these traits lies in the fact that the Sheltie is still used today for herding and droving in the British Isles, the Shetland Islands and America. Sheepgrowers in the western United States—Montana, Utah, Colorado and Idaho, for example—employ Shelties because they cover ground so well and experience little difficulty in working in snow country. Their light weight prevents them from sink-

ing deep into the snow as they drive the flocks. In addition, Shelties are found to be more gentle with ewes at lambing time than some of the larger herding dogs.

Though the Shetland Sheepdog is an ancient breed, as evidenced by literature and art, the breed has managed to keep up with its master's changing lifestyles. A perfect example of this modern Sheltie phenomenon is a lovely little bitch named Tassie. Her story exemplifies the intelligence and versatility of Shelties and epitomises the dogs' dedication to their masters.

Today Tassie lives in the tropical state of Florida with her owner, Bert Jenks. Until she retired, Tassie's life was anything but casual or leisurely. Jenks and his wife, Joan, lived on a 36,000-acre ranch in the rolling hills of Central Colorado at the foot of the Rocky Moun-

Tassie, working a herd of yearling cattle on a ranch in Colorado, USA. Tassie is owned by Bert Jenks; Joan Jenks took the photo.

Tassie, besides being a successful herder of young cattle, is also a very beautiful dog. She resides happily with her owners Bert and Joan Jenks in their retirement home in Florida, USA.

tains in the Western US. Rolling High Jenks Ranch was a 52-square-mile cattle ranch. The mountain peaks that surround the ranch reach heights of 14,000 feet.

Tassie was purchased by the Jenks in Florida, where they spend the winter months on the small island called Sanibel in the Gulf of Mexico, off Florida's western coast. When spring arrived and Tassie was a mere six months old, the Jenks packed up and returned to their cattle farm. At the time, the Jenks' house was not surrounded by a protective fence so all

manner of wildlife made a habit of foraging on the flowers in Joan's beds. Squirrels, rabbits, antelope and deer were regular unwelcome visitors.

Every day Bert would take Tassie with him to work the cattle and whenever he was home, he and Tassie would chase off the wildlife in the garden. Out on the range, Tassie worked with a part-dingo dog named Buddy. Lessons from Buddy plus her natural instincts for herding taught Tassie how to move the cattle at the direction of the cowboys. Because she was so small, Tassie was usually

17

assigned to work the yearling cattle, both heifers and steers. Though these animals weigh an average of 600 pounds each, Tassie quickly learned to stay out of their way whilst at the same time remaining close enough to move them according to the voice and hand signals of the herdsmen.

Tassie's life took on a regular rhythm of working cattle in Colorado and wintering in Florida with her owners. Whilst in Florida, Tassie's life was not without purpose, however. She and Jenks enroled in an obedience class and Tassie's formal education became a reality.

Shelties are easily trained for agility exercises such as jumping through a hoop. Shelties make excellent candidates for agility and obedience trials.

Following basic obedience training, Bert and Tassie moved up the ranks of various levels of difficulty until they reached the level known as 'Skills.' In the Skills class, Tassie developed distance control, hand signals, retrieving, jumping and scent discrimination, including narcotics detection. In other words, Tassie had reached the peak of canine performance and done it with ease.

All the while Tassie was perfecting her training in winter, she continued herding cattle and chasing off wildlife around her home in summer. At night, regardless of where she was, she would sleep beside Bert's bed and keep watch over the house.

At age eight years, Tassie, along with her family, left the ranch they loved and retired to Florida. She still works out each week with her Skills class and has joined a dog-owner dance team.

Tassie proves an interesting theory: A dog with strong genetic factors for certain behaviours can be transported to an artificial environment and still exhibit those traits. Tassie, through hundreds of years of genetic breeding for herding, retains the herding instinct whilst at the same time adapts to a completely different lifestyle and excels at both. Further proof of the power of genetics and controlled breeding seems unnecessary.

Whether Shetland Sheepdogs are bred for showing, herding or pet life, their natural instincts remain intact.

Personality of the
SHETLAND SHEEPDOG

The Shetland Sheepdog's unique heritage has given it certain qualities that endear it to modern owners around the world. As we've seen, genetics is what it's all about and the particular behavioural traits bred into the Sheltie so many years ago have given it the ability to adapt so successfully to modern-day living.

For example, their intelligence and natural tendency to obey with a minimum amount of training gives them a decided advantage in today's busy lifestyle, and in various dog activities such as obedience and agility competition. Their grace, speed and nimbleness carry over from

their lives on the range to today's farm work and recreational activities such as agility trials, jumping and other sports. They are, in fact, one of the most popular breeds used in obedience trials.

Their watchdog instincts makes them great alarm dogs around home and property just as it did in guarding flocks against poachers and predators. Their docile nature coupled with a keen awareness of their environment makes them perfect family companions. Their devotion to family makes them a pleasure to live with and a joy to train.

Because of this devotion factor, Shelties are best obtained as puppies rather than mature adults since, as adults, they have most likely bonded strong-

Did You Know?

Shelties love children and will spend their waking hours trying to gather their 'flock' together in one room rather than being scattered throughout the house. Since the children of the family are the Sheltie's chosen flock, the Sheltie feels a great responsibility for their safety and keeping them close together.

Intelligence, friendly temperament, working ability and beauty—the Shetland Sheepdog is a breed that has it all.

ly with their first owners. The transition to another owner later in life can prove extremely stressful. Sheltie owners have often told how their dogs sulk or yearn for them when they go away.

Shelties make ideal family pets and are very tolerant of all children. Actually, they love little children and usually watch

Did You Know?

Due to the heavy coat of the Sheltie, he can withstand cold climates very easily. However, that same coat requires daily brushing and owners must expect heavy moulting at least once a year. If you don't like brushing a dog—or are allergic to dog hair—seek a different breed.

21

Shelties make wonderful pets, especially when brought home as a puppy and allowed to bond with all family members.

is best limited by teaching the dog not to bark excessively at an early age. Allow the dog to warn you of visitors to your home, but discourage unnecessary barking, for example, when he's excited about something or in anticipation of dinnertime or friends' calling in for a visit.

Shelties are busy dogs. They do not enjoy being left around the house with nothing to do or forced to be inactive for too long. They can become distressed and neurotic. They need daily exercise and weekly physical activities that get them outdoors and doing things such as hiking, long walks in the park, jogging with owners, etc. Remember this is a dog bred to run for miles each day without tiring: a two-mile run will hardly be considered a challenge!

The Shetland Sheepdog's perception of his owner's moods is remarkable. They sense all

over them like a nanny. Owners must be mindful, however, of tiny infants and toddlers who may wobble and fall on the dog, causing injury to the dog.

Owners will often observe their Sheltie trying to round up the children as if they were its own little flock of sheep! They like to see their human family members clustered together rather than separated and apart from one another.

Shelties can also be very vocal. With a high-pitched bark they express frustrations, concern, excitement and even calls for attention. This vocalisation

Did You Know?

In many countries, young Shelties are first trained to herd on ducks. Since the ducks easily cluster together and can be moved in a tight flock from one place to another, the Shelties manage the birds more easily than sheep during the learning process. In South Africa, because of their larger size, Collies are used to herd ostriches.

manner of human emotions and react accordingly. They worry with the sad owner, celebrate with the excited, happy one and so on. Actually dogs are much like humans when it comes to emotions: they experience many of the same emotions as humans.

The ideal Sheltie owner is an active person who enjoys working with his dog, teaching him new things and going places and doing things together. He is a person who also enjoys the few minutes each day required to keep the Sheltie's coat free of matts and looking clean. A person who enjoys outdoor activities in all seasons makes a good candidate for Sheltie companionship. Because of the dog's love of master and family, a Sheltie owner must be a demonstrative person who will give love and enjoy receiving the love of a Sheltie.

One final word about the ideal owner of a Shetland

Shelties make ideal companions for children of all ages. It is of course essential that the children understand how to treat a dog so that mutual respect is established.

Did You Know?

The Sheltie is a calm, dignified dog that does not take well to unpredictable owners. Rough and erratic training methods are not successful with Shelties. These herding dogs respond best to patient, gentle training methods and, because of their intelligence, learn quickly and eagerly.

Sheepdog: Due to the dog's intelligence and love of physical activity, Shelties should be trained at an early age. They love learning and are quick to conceptualise behaviours. They willingly practise a particular behaviour several times with the owner and then suddenly refuse to repeat the behaviour again. From those few repetitions, they learn the desired behaviour and practising too many times proves boring to them. It's their way of saying, 'You showed me what to do. I've done it. Now

23

Shelties are digni-
fied, clever dogs
that can adapt
quickly to family
life. Many Sheltie
owners are amazed
at how easily their
dogs are trained.

The pastoral dogs, designed to respond to a shepherd's command and hand signal, are among the brightest of all canines. The Shetland Sheepdog, with its amenable disposition, leaps to the head of the class.

Did You Know?

Shyness, timidity, stubbornness, snappiness and bad temper are all considered major faults in Shetland Sheepdogs. They must be avoided at all costs to preserve true Sheltie temperament.

let's do something else. This is boring.'

The next day the owner will be amazed to see that the dog remembers the behaviours and performs them to perfection upon hearing the command. They truly are one of the world's brightest canine students.

25

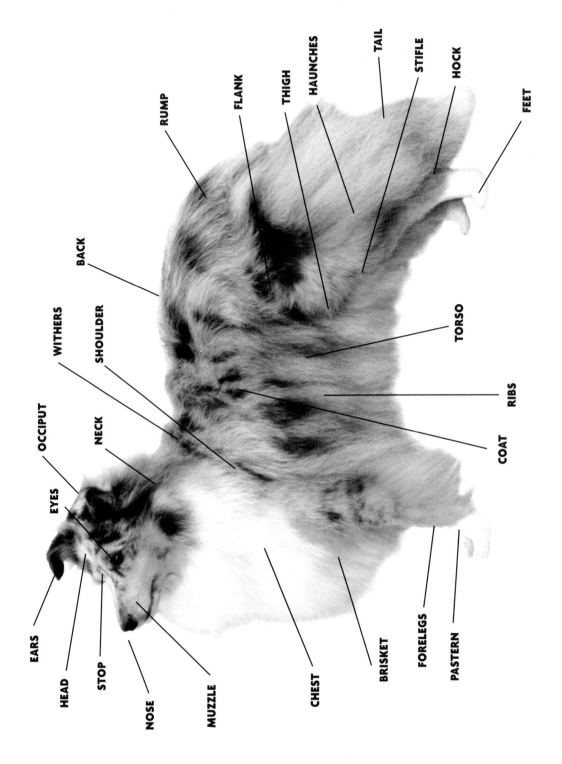

Breed Standard for the
SHETLAND SHEEPDOG

The Sheltie is a small, robust dog, well rounded in appearance with no sharp angles or rigid lines when viewed from front or back. He wears a rough longhaired outer coat with a soft, dense undercoat to provide warmth in cold climates. The soft, furry undercoat must be so thick that it forces the harsh outer coat to stand up rather than lay flat against the body.

In males, the mane should be particularly abundant and impressive. Both sexes sport a large wide collar of fur around the neck often referred to as the ruff. Overall the Sheltie presents a symmetrical appearance with the males being masculine and the females obviously feminine.

Coat colours are varied enough to please the most discriminating human taste. Black, blue merle and sable, ranging from golden tones to deep mahogany, are the colour choices. Small amounts of white are permitted but more than 50 percent white is considered a fault in the show ring.

Fore and hind legs carry ample feathering down to the hock joint (ankle). Below that, the hair is short and smooth against the skin. The tail is a large full plume that the dog carries low

when at rest and extended when he's working or running. Hair on the face, ears and feet should be short and smooth. For show purposes, the hair on these parts may be trimmed to present a clean look.

The dogs should weigh 25 to 30 pounds and stand about 14 inches at the shoulder. Males are slightly larger than females. The breed standard used for judging the breed in the country of its birth will also dictate size and height.

Keeping in mind that the Shetland Sheepdog should give the appearance of a Collie in

In order for a dog to win his class, the Breed, and the show, it must impress the judges as the closest to the standard of all dogs entered that day. This Best in Show winner conforms closely with the standard.

miniature, any deviation from that look should be considered a serious fault in the show ring. That 'Collie look' has dominated the breed for centuries—it must be fostered in every future generation. The breed standard is designed to ensure that it does.

A breed standard is a word picture of the ideal dog of a particular breed. The breed standard for the Shetland Sheepdog spells out what the dog should look like in detail. Features such as size, proportion, substance, head, neck, body, forequarters, hindquarters, coat, gait and temperament are all addressed in the standard.

The standard in each country varies slightly so it's important to familiarise yourself with the standard of perfection for the Shetland Sheepdog in your country. In Britain, of course, the standard used is the standard recognised by The Kennel Club, which sets the wording of the standard and then relies on its auspices to enforce it. Breed clubs follow the direction of The Kennel Club in enforcing its standard. In some countries, the breed clubs set the standards and submit them to the national club for approval. This is how such matters are handled in the US, for example.

In addition to specific standards for physical characteristics, the standard also spells out faults, both physical and temperamental, that demerit the dog if any of those traits are present. Some breed standards also include disqualifications, which forbid the dog from competing in a show when the judge acknowledges the standard. For example, the American standard states that a short, choppy gait with stiff, jerky movements is a serious fault.

The reason that gait is considered so important in the Sheltie is that traditionally the dog must travel many miles in a day as he herds cattle or sheep. Anything less than lithe, smooth and graceful movement—in essence, effortless—would tire the dog so severely that he could not perform his job. Thus, he would not be considered an ideal Sheltie.

Atop the magnificently coated body is the distinctive shape of the Sheltie's head. A flat skull tapering into a blunt, wedge-shaped head from ears to black nose must not be sharp nor snipy. Small ears are carried erect and the tips should fall forward.

Without that special Collie look of the head and ears, a Sheltie would hardly be called a Shetland Sheepdog. Eyes are almond-shaped and dark in colour. Only the blue merles are permitted to have blue eyes.

Overall expression of the Sheltie is one of curiosity and intelligent alertness. The head is always carried proudly. The expression toward strangers should be of watchful reserve; he is never fearful or nervous.

An handsome Best in Show winner showing off a keen expression, a luxurious coat and an ideal Sheltie head. Shelties are popular choices for Best in Show since they are crowd-pleasers and love to perform.

In summary the breed standard spells out exactly what a particular breed should and should not be. It provides the guidelines for breeders to follow in producing today's dogs and ensuring the blueprints of tomorrow's generations of purebred dogs.

THE KENNEL CLUB STANDARD FOR THE SHETLAND SHEEPDOG

General Appearance: Small, long-haired working dog of great beauty, free from cloddiness and coarseness. Outline symmetrical so that no part appears out of proportion to whole. Abundant coat, mane and frill, shapeliness of head and sweetness of expression combine to present the ideal.

Characteristics: Alert, gentle, intelligent, strong and active.

Temperament: Affectionate and responsive to his owner, reserved towards strangers, never nervous.

Head and Skull: Head refined; when viewed from top or side a long, blunt wedge, tapering from ear to nose. Width of skull in proportion to length of skull and muzzle. Whole to be considered in connection with size of dog. Skull flat, moderately wide dividing between ears, with no prominence of occipital bone. Cheeks flat, merging smoothly into well rounded muzzle. Skull and muzzle

CORRECT EARS THAT TIP FORWARD

INCORRECT EARS

zle of equal length, dividing point inner corner of eye. Topline of skull parallel to topline of muzzle, with slight by definite stop. Nose, lips and eye rims black. The characteristic expression is obtained by the perfect balance and combination of skull and foreface, shape, colour and placement of eyes, correct position and carriage of ears.

Eyes: Medium size obliquely set, almond-shape. Dark brown except in the case of merles, where one or both may be blue or blue-flecked.

GOOD NOSE

INCORRECT NOSE

Ears: Small, moderately wide at base, placed fairly close together on top of skull. In repose, thrown back; when alert brought forward and carried semi-erect with tips falling forward.

Mouth: Jaws level, clean, strong with well-developed underjaw. Lips tight. Teeth sound with a perfect, regular and complete scissor bite, i.e., upper teeth closely overlapping lower teeth and set square to the jaws. A full complement of 42 properly placed teeth highly desired.

Neck: Muscular, well arched, of sufficient length to carry head proudly.

Forequarters: Shoulders very well laid back. At withers, separated only by vertebrae, but blades sloping outwards to accommodate desired spring of ribs. Shoulder joint well angled. Upper arm and shoulder blade approximately equal in length. Elbow equidistant from ground and withers. Forelegs straight when viewed from front, muscular and clean with strong bone. Pasterns strong and flexible.

Body: Slightly longer from point of shoulder to bottom of croup than height at withers. Chest deep, reaching to point of elbow. Ribs well sprung, tapering at lower half to allow free play of forelegs and shoulders. Back level,

31

with graceful sweep over loins, croup slopes gradually to rear.

Hindquarters: Thigh broad and muscular, thigh bones set into pelvis at right angles. Stifle joint has distinct angle, hock joint clean cut, angular, well let down with strong bone. Hocks straight when viewed from behind.

Feet: Oval soles, well padded, toes arched and close together.

Tail: Set low; tapering bone reaches to at least hock; with abundant hair and slight upward sweep. May be slightly raised when moving but never over level of back. Never kinked.

Gait/Movement: Lithe, smooth and graceful with drive from hindquarters, covering the maximum amount of ground with minimum of effort. Pacing, plaiting, rolling, or stiff, stilted, up and down movement highly undesirable.

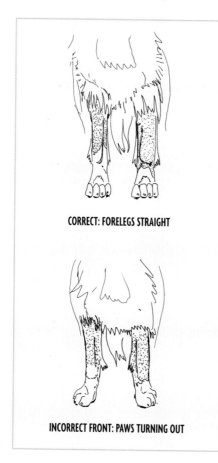

CORRECT: FORELEGS STRAIGHT

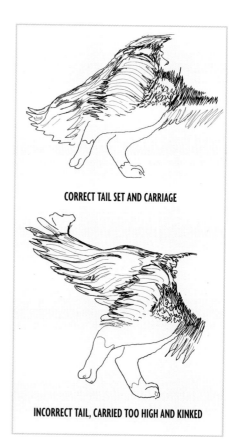

CORRECT TAIL SET AND CARRIAGE

INCORRECT FRONT: PAWS TURNING OUT

INCORRECT TAIL, CARRIED TOO HIGH AND KINKED

CORRECT COAT WITH MANE AND FRILL

COAT TOO SPARSE

Coat: Double; outer coat of long hair, harsh-textured and straight. Undercoat soft, short and close. Mane and frill very abundant, forelegs well feathered. Hindlegs above hocks profusely covered with hair, below hocks fairly smooth. Face smooth. Smooth-coated specimens highly undesirable.

Colour: Sable—clear or shaded, any colour from pale gold to deep mahogany, in its shade, rich in tone. Wolf-sable and grey undesirable.

Tricolour—intense black on body, rich tan markings preferred.

Blue Merle—clear silvery blue, splashed and marbled with black. Rich tan marking preferred but absence not penalised. Heavy black markings, slate or rusty tinge in either top or undercoat highly undesirable; general effect must be blue.

Black and White, and Black and Tan: also recognised colours.

White markings may appear (except on black and tan) in blaze, collar and chest, frill, legs and tip of tail. All or some white markings are preferred (except on black and tan) but absence of these markings not to be penalised. Patches of white on body highly undesirable.

Size: Ideal height at withers: dogs: 37 cms (14.5 ins); bitches: 35.5. cms (14 ins). More than 2.5 cms (1 in) above or below these heights highly undesirable.

Faults: Any departure from the foregoing points should be considered a fault and the seriousness with which the fault should be regarded should be in exact proportion to its degree.

Note: Male animals should have two apparently normal testicles fully descended into the scrotum.

SHETLAND SHEEPDOG

You should acquire your Sheltie puppy from a good breeder with an established reputation. Puppies at just four weeks of age are beginning to display their individual personalities.

WHERE TO BEGIN?

We've already talked about serious health problems to consider when choosing a Sheltie puppy. If a breeder ignores your questions about certifying his breeding stock from congenital diseases, no matter his reasoning, find another breeder. Every reputable breeder is concerned about his dogs' health and genetic contributions to future generations. He makes every effort to be well informed about the breed's health problems and veterinary science's role in curing and/or prevent such problems in the future. A good breeder will be eager to explain health concerns to you and share whatever knowledge he has in regards to his breeding stock. He will also be anxious to share with you the name and address of their vet whom you may want to speak with concerning the parents of the litter.

In addition to major health concerns, there are other considerations to be aware of in the acquiring of a puppy. Here are some things to think about:

1. When you arrive at the location of the puppies, look around the place before you even look at the litter. Is it clean? Is there a place for the puppies to play, eat, sleep, or are they crowded in a small space on newspaper?

2. When you first see the litter, do the puppies come running to you in friendly anticipation or

Did You Know?

Your selection of a good puppy can be determined by your needs. A show potential or a good pet? It is your choice. Every puppy, however, should be of good temperament. Although show-quality puppies are bred and raised with emphasis on physical conformation, responsible breeders strive for equally good temperament. Do not buy from a breeder who concentrates solely on physical beauty at the expense of personality.

do they run away and cringe in fear?

3. What about the parents? Are they well cared for and clean? Are they friendly, standoffish or aggressive? You should know that the temperament of the parents is probably what the puppies will be like when they grow up. By all means, puppies should be especially friendly and happy with little or no sense of protectiveness at early ages.

4. No doubt you will have an opportunity to observe some puppy faeces. Is the stool well formed and solid? Loose, runny stools are a cause for concern and should be checked by a vet who will be looking for the cause such as worms, infection, bacterial infestations, etc.

5. How do the puppies interact with owner? They should not show fear but instead by happy to see him or her and anxious for attention. If you observe one particular puppy sitting off in a corner by himself, that puppy is not a good candidate for you: it will

probably grow up to be shy, perhaps even a fear-biter.

6. As your eyes (and your heart) gravitate toward one particular puppy, take a careful look at it. Is it clean? Does it smell good with a sweet, puppy breath? Are its eyes bright and shiny, its nose cool and not running? Is it coughing? Does it have fleas or any other parasites?

7. Check out the sex of the puppies that you are interested in.

It is ideal to see the dam with her litter. By meeting the dam, you can better assess the temperament of the litter as well as the eventual size of the pups.

The dam should be approachable and eager to meet you. She may be somewhat protective of her pups at first, but eventually should allow you to meet them and become acquainted.

Before you began your search, you should have decided which sex was best for you and your family. Keep in mind that male dogs should be castrated and female dogs spayed at the appropriate age. Discuss the age and the advantages of neutering with your veterinary surgeon.

8. Finally, does the breeder have the proper registration papers for The Kennel Club to go with the puppy of your choice? The breeder should also provide you with a feeding schedule and

whatever else you need to make the puppy's transition from birth home to your home as easy and stress-free as possible. A pedigree is also a desirable document to get with your puppy. Tracing the history of your puppy's family, the pedigree tells you the registered names of parents, grandparents and great-grandparents on both the puppy's sire's and dam's sides. It also documents any degrees and/or titles those relatives might have earned, which can help you understand the physical conformation and/or training accomplishments of your pup's relatives.

If you have intentions of your new charge herding sheep, there are many more considerations. The parents of a future working dog should have excellent qualifications, including actual work experience as well as working titles in their pedigrees. Working Shelties are less common than, say, working Border Collies, but it is not impossible to acquire such a dog. By and large, the breed still maintains its working instincts. Look in farming newspapers and journals to find the Shetland Sheepdogs that are trained and bred for working purposes.

Breeders commonly allow visitors to see the litter by around the fifth or sixth week, and puppies leave for their new homes between the eighth and tenth week. Breeders who permit their puppies to leave early are more

Did You Know?

Your puppy should have a well-fed appearance but not a distended abdomen, which may indicate worms or incorrect feeding, or both. The body should be firm, with a solid feel. The skin of the abdomen should be pale pink and clean, without signs of scratching or rash. Check the hind legs to make certain that dewclaws were removed, if any were present at birth.

interested in your pounds than their puppies' well being. Puppies need to learn the rules of the trade from their dams, and most dams continue teaching the pups manners, and dos and don'ts until around the eighth week. Breeders spend significant amounts of time with the Shetland Sheepdog toddlers so that they are able to interact with the 'other species', i.e., humans. Given the long history that dogs and humans have, bonding between the two species is natural but must be nurtured. A

Your Schedule . . .

If you lead an erratic, unpredictable life, with daily or weekly changes in your work requirements, consider the problems of owning a puppy. The new puppy has to be fed regularly, socialised (loved, petted, handled, introduced to other people) and, most importantly, allowed to visit outdoors for toilet training. As the dog gets older, it can be more tolerant of deviations in its feeding and toilet relief.

The puppies should stay with the dam until they are about eight weeks old. Their mother's milk is also a necessity during their growth period from birth to at least four weeks of age.

well-bred, well-socialised Shetland Sheepdog pup wants nothing more than to be near you and please you.

COMMITMENT OF OWNERSHIP

After considering all of these factors, you have most likely already made some very important decisions about selecting your puppy. You have chosen a Shetland Sheepdog, which means that you have decided which characteristics you want in a dog and what type of dog will best fit into your family and lifestyle. If you have selected a breeder, you have gone a step further—you have done your research and found a responsible, conscientious person who breeds quality Shetland Sheepdogs and who should be a reliable source of help as you and your puppy adjust to life together. If you have observed a litter in action, you have obtained a first-hand look at the dynamics of a puppy 'pack' and, thus, you should learn about each pup's individual personality—perhaps you have even found one that particularly appeals to you.

However, even if you have not yet found the Shetland Sheepdog puppy of your dreams, observing pups will help you learn to recognise certain behaviour and to determine what a pup's behaviour indicates about his temperament. You will be able to pick out which pups are the leaders, which ones are less outgoing, which ones are confident, which ones are shy, playful, friendly, aggressive, etc. Equally as important, you will learn to recognise what a healthy pup should look and act like. All of these things will help you in your search, and when you find the Shetland Sheepdog that was meant for you, you will know it!

Boy or Girl?

An important consideration to be discussed is the sex of your puppy. For a family companion, a bitch may be the better choice, considering the female's inbred concern for all young creatures and her accompanying tolerance and patience. It is always advised to spay a pet bitch, which may guarantee her a longer life.

Gentle handling and human interaction from an early age helps puppies grow up to be well adjusted.

Researching your breed, selecting a responsible breeder and observing as many pups as possible are all important steps on the way to dog ownership. It may seem like a lot of effort…and you have not even brought the pup home yet! Remember, though, you cannot be too careful when it comes to deciding on the type of dog you want and finding out about your prospective pup's background. Buying a puppy is not—or should not be—just another whimsical purchase. This is one instance in which you actually do get to choose your own family! You may be thinking that buying a puppy should be fun—it should not be so serious and so much work. Keep in mind that your puppy is not a cuddly stuffed toy or decorative lawn ornament, but a creature that will become a real member of your family. You will come to realise that, whilst buying a puppy is a pleasurable and exciting endeavour, it is not something to be taken lightly. Relax…the fun will start when the pup comes home!

Always keep in mind that a puppy is nothing more than a baby in a furry disguise…a baby

who is virtually helpless in a human world and who trusts his owner for fulfilment of his basic needs for survival. In addition to water and shelter, your pup needs

Documentation

Two important documents you will get from the breeder are the pup's pedigree and registration papers. The breeder should register the litter and each pup with The Kennel Club, and it is necessary for you to have the paperwork if you plan on showing or breeding in the future.

Make sure you know the breeder's intentions on which type of registration he will obtain for the pup. There are limited registrations which may prohibit the dog from being shown or from competing in non-conformation trials such as Working or Agility if the breeder feels that the pup is not of sufficient quality to do so. There is also a type of registration that will permit the dog in non-conformation competition only.

If your dog is registered with a Kennel-Club-recognised breed club, then you can register the pup with The Kennel Club yourself. Your breeder can assist you with the specifics of the registration process.

Breeders introduce toys to the litter as a part of socialisation. Be advised not to offer your puppy toys designed for humans. Dog toys are a speciality that must be obtained from pet shop or supply store.

PREPARING PUPPY'S PLACE IN YOUR HOME

Researching your breed and finding a breeder are only two aspects of the 'homework' you will have to do before bringing your Shetland Sheepdog puppy home. You will also have to prepare your home and family for the new addition. Much as you would prepare a nursery for a newborn baby, you will need to designate a care, protection, guidance and love. If you are not prepared to commit to this, then you are not prepared to own a dog.

Wait a minute, you say. How hard could this be? All of my neighbours own dogs and they seem to be doing just fine. Why should I have to worry about all of this? Well, you should not worry about it; in fact, you will probably find that once your Shetland Sheepdog pup gets used to his new home, he will fall into his place in the family quite naturally. But it never hurts to emphasise the commitment of dog ownership. With some time and patience, it is really not too difficult to raise a curious and exuberant Shetland Sheepdog pup to be a well-adjusted and well-mannered adult dog—a dog that could be your most loyal friend.

Often times an owner can choose a puppy before the pup is old enough to leave the breeder. The breeder will 'hold' the puppy until the pup is a proper age to go to his new home.

Do Your Homework!

Unfortunately, when a puppy is bought by someone who does not take into consideration the time and attention that dog ownership requires, it is the puppy who suffers when he is either abandoned or placed in a shelter by a frustrated owner. So all of the 'homework' you do in preparation for your pup's arrival will benefit you both. The more informed you are, the more you will know what to expect and the better equipped you will be to handle the ups and downs of raising a puppy. Hopefully, everyone in the household is willing to do his part in raising and caring for the pup. The anticipation of owning a dog often brings a lot of promises from excited family members: 'I will walk him every day,' 'I will feed him,' 'I will housebreak him,' etc., but these things take time and effort, and promises can easily be forgotten once the novelty of the new pet has worn off.

41

Your Sheltie puppy will adapt quickly to his new environment and make himself feel at home. Establish the house rules immediately and be consistent. Will he or will he not be allowed on the furniture?

place in your home that will be the puppy's own. How you prepare your home will depend on how much freedom the dog will be allowed. Whatever you decide,

Insurance

Many good breeders will offer you insurance with your new puppy, which is an excellent idea. The first few weeks of insurance will probably be covered free of charge or with only minimal cost, allowing you to take up the policy when this expires. If you own a pet dog, it is sensible to take out such a policy as veterinary fees can be high, although routine vaccinations and boosters are not covered. Look carefully at the many options open to you before deciding which suits you best.

you must ensure that he has a place that he can 'call his own.'

When you bring your new puppy into your home, you are bringing him into what will become his home as well. Obviously, you did not buy a puppy so that he could take over your house, but in order for a puppy to grow into a stable, well-adjusted dog, he has to feel comfortable in his surroundings. Remember, he is leaving the warmth and security of his mother and littermates, as well as the familiarity of the only place he has ever known, so it is important to make his transition as easy as possible. By preparing a place in your home for the puppy, you are making him feel as welcome as possible in a strange new place. It should not take him long to get used to it, but the sudden shock of being transplanted is somewhat traumatic for a young pup. Imagine how a small child would feel in the same situation— that is how your puppy must be feeling. It is up to you to reassure him and to let him know, 'Little fellow, you are going to like it here!'

WHAT YOU SHOULD BUY
CRATE
To someone unfamiliar with the use of crates in dog training, it may seem like punishment to shut a dog in a crate, but this is not the case at all. Although all breeders do not advocate crate training,

more and more breeders and trainers are recommending crates as a preferred tool for show puppies as well as pet puppies. Crates are not cruel—crates have many humane and highly effective uses in dog care and training. For example, crate training is a very popular and very successful housebreaking method. A crate can keep your dog safe during travel; and, perhaps most importantly, a crate provides your dog with a place of his own in your home.

Crate training should be amongst an owner's first considerations with a new Sheltie. Teaching the dog or puppy to enjoy using his crate offers protection from all manner of injuries to the dog to say nothing of keeping your home safe from puppy destruction. Having his own crate provides security for the dog and

Be sure that the crate your purchase for your Sheltie will be large enough to accommodate the dog at his adult size.

gives him a safe place to stay whilst you are out of the home and unable to supervise him. A common complaint for pet owners is the dog that literally destroys the house whenever he is left alone. This is called isolation frustration and occurs when the dog is given too much freedom without human supervision. The solution to the problem is offering a place of security to the dog so that he has no need to be anxious about being alone. This little den is the answer.

Many dogs sleep in their crates overnight. When lined with soft bedding and a favourite toy, a crate becomes a cosy pseudo-den for your dog. Like his ancestors, he too will seek out the comfort and retreat of a den—you just happen to be providing him with something a little more luxurious than his early ancestors enjoyed.

As far as purchasing a crate,

Did You Know?

The majority of problems that are commonly seen in young pups will disappear as your dog gets older. However, how you deal with problems when he is young will determine how he reacts to discipline as an adult dog. It is important to establish who is boss (hopefully it will be you!) right away when you are first bonding with your dog. This bond will set the tone for the rest of your life together.

43

Buy your necessities before you bring your puppy home. Your local pet shop will usually have everything you require.

open, allowing the air to flow through and affording the dog a view of what is going on around him whilst a fibreglass crate is sturdier. Both can double as travel crates, providing protection for the dog. The size of the crate is another thing to consider. Since Shelties are smallish dogs, a medium-size crate will be necessary for a full-grown Shetland Sheepdog, who stands approximately 14 inches high.

GATES

Whilst on the subject of housing, let's talk about baby gates. These low dividers are primarily manufactured for use in keeping children confined to certain areas of the home. However, they are equally effective in confining dogs to certain rooms as well. When you're housebreaking a puppy,

the type that you buy is up to you. It will most likely be one of the two most popular types: wire or fibreglass. There are advantages and disadvantages to each type. For example, a wire crate is more

Did You Know?

You should not even think about buying a puppy that looks sick, undernourished, overly frightened or nervous. Sometimes a timid puppy will warm up to you after a 30-minute 'let's-get-acquainted' session.

Did You Know?

Taking your dog from the breeder to your home in a car can be a very uncomfortable experience for both of you. The puppy will have been taken from his warm, friendly, safe environment and brought into a strange new environment. An environment that moves! Be prepared for loose bowels, urination, crying, whining and even fear biting. With proper love and encouragement when you arrive home, the stress of the trip should quickly disappear.

you will be more successful if he's limited to small areas where you can keep an eye on him until he's completely reliable regarding his toilet training (usually until about six months of age).

BEDDING
Veterinary bedding in the dog's crate will help the dog feel more

Did You Know?

The cost of food must also be mentioned. All dogs need a good quality food with an adequate supply of protein to develop their bones and muscles properly. Most dogs are not picky eaters but unless fed properly they can quickly succumb to skin problems.

at home and you may also like to pop in a small blanket. This will take the place of the leaves, twigs, etc., that the pup would use in the wild to make a den; the pup can make his own 'burrow' in the crate. Although your pup is far removed from his den-making ancestors, the denning instinct is still a part of his genetic makeup.

PHOTO COURTESY OF DOSKOCIL.

Second, until you bring your pup home, he has been sleeping amidst the warmth of his mother and littermates, and whilst a blanket is not the same as a warm,

Show dogs absolutely must be crate trained. Crates are ideal for travel to and from the shows and for accommodation whilst the Sheltie awaits his turn in the ring.

Your local pet shop will have various sizes, colours and types of dog crates available for your selection. The shopkeeper can assist you in selecting a crate ideal for your Sheltie.

45

A wire pen gives the puppies sunshine and exercise whilst confined outdoors. Breeders and exhibitors commonly use these, though such a playpen is not sturdy or large enough for regular use.

breathing body, it still provides heat and something with which to snuggle. You will want to wash your pup's bedding frequently in case he has an accident in his crate, and replace or remove any blanket that becomes ragged and starts to fall apart.

Toys

Toys are a must for dogs of all ages, especially for curious playful pups. Puppies are the 'children' of the dog world, and what child does not love toys? Chew toys provide enjoyment to both dog and owner—your dog will enjoy playing with his favourite toys, whilst you will enjoy the fact that they distract him from

Crate Training Tips

During crate training, you should partition off the section of the crate in which the pup stays. If he is given too big an area, this will hinder your training efforts. Crate training is based on the fact that a dog does not like to soil his sleeping quarters, so it is ineffective to keep a pup in a crate that is so big that he can eliminate in one end and get far enough away from it to sleep. Also, you want to make the crate den-like for the pup. Blankets and a favourite toy will make the crate cosy for the small pup; as he grows, you may want to evict some of his 'roommates' to make more room.

It will take some coaxing at first, but be patient. Given some time to get used to it, your pup will adapt to his new home-within-a-home quite nicely.

Be certain that your Sheltie's outdoor accommodations are secure. Gates must close completely and lock for the safety of your Shelties.

A small gate is no match for a curious Sheltie pup! Make sure the gate you select is tall enough to keep your Sheltie safely confined.

de-stuffed in no time. The overly excited pup may ingest the stuffing, which is neither digestible nor nutritious.

Similarly, squeaky toys are quite popular, but must be avoided for the Shetland Sheepdog. Perhaps a squeaky toy can be used as an aid in training, but not for free play. If a pup 'disembowels' one of these, the small plastic squeaker inside can be dangerous if swallowed. Monitor the condition of all your pup's toys carefully and get rid of any that have been chewed to the point of becoming potentially dangerous.

Be careful of natural bones, which have a tendency to splinter into sharp, dangerous pieces. Also be careful of rawhide, which can turn into pieces that are easy to swallow or into a mushy mess on your carpet.

your expensive shoes and leather sofa. Puppies love to chew; in fact, chewing is a physical need for pups as they are teething, and everything looks appetising! The full range of your possessions—from old dishcloth to Oriental rug—are fair game in the eyes of a teething pup. Puppies are not all that discerning when it comes to finding something to literally 'sink their teeth into'—everything tastes great!

Shetland Sheepdog puppies are fairly aggressive chewers and only the hardest, strongest toys should be offered to them. Breeders advise owners to resist stuffed toys, because they can become

Electrical Fencing

The electrical fencing system which forms an invisible fence works on a battery-operated collar that shocks the dog if it gets too close to the buried (or elevated) wire. There are some people who think very highly of this system of controlling a dog's wandering. Keep in mind that the collar has batteries. For safety's sake, replace the batteries every month with the best quality batteries available.

47

Tug toys are extremely popular with Shelties. Only use ropes made especially for dogs and with non-toxic dyes.

Toys, Toys, Toys!

With a big variety of dog toys available, and so many that look like they would be a lot of fun for a dog, be careful in your selection. It is amazing what a set of puppy teeth can do to an innocent-looking toy, so, obviously, safety is a major consideration. Be sure to choose the most durable products that you can find. Hard nylon bones and toys are a safe bet, and many of them are offered in different scents and flavours that will be sure to capture your dog's attention. It is always fun to play a game of catch with your dog, and there are balls and flying discs that are specially made to withstand dog teeth.

LEAD

A nylon lead is probably the best option as it is the most resistant to puppy teeth should your pup take a liking to chewing on his lead. Of course, this is a habit that should be nipped in the bud, but if your pup likes to chew on his lead he has a very slim chance of being able to chew through the strong nylon. Nylon leads are also lightweight, which is good for a young Shetland Sheepdog who is just getting used to the idea of walking on a lead. For everyday walking and safety purposes, the nylon lead is a good choice. As your pup grows up and gets used to walking on the lead, you may want to purchase a flexible lead. These leads allow you to extend the length to give the dog a broader area to explore or to shorten the length to keep the dog close to you. Of course there are special leads for training purposes, and specially made leather harnesses for the working Shetland Sheepdogs, but these are not necessary for routine walks.

Only offer your Sheltie toys that are made especially for dogs. Dog toys are available at most pet shops.

COLLAR

Your pup should get used to wearing a collar all the time since you will want to attach his ID tags to it. Also, you have to attach the lead to something! A lightweight nylon collar is a good choice; make sure that it fits snugly enough so that the pup cannot wriggle out of it, but is loose enough so that it will not be uncomfortably tight around the pup's neck. You should be able to fit a finger between the pup and the collar. It may take some time for your pup to get used to wearing the collar, but soon he will not even notice that it is there. The snap collars are handy and easy to use. Buckle collars are also suitable but can get entangled in the dog's fur when you put on the collar. A chain collar is not necessary for any puppy nor adult Shelties. They are more than willing to stay by your side and not pull when you walk together. It's truly the Sheltie's nature to heel.

Pet shops usually stock large quantities of dog leads. Select the lead that suits your taste and pocketbook. The Sheltie does not require a very heavy lead.

Did You Know?

It will take at least two weeks for your puppy to become accustomed to his new surroundings. Give him lots of love, attention, handling, frequent opportunities to relieve himself, a diet he likes to eat and a place he can call his own.

FOOD AND WATER BOWLS

Your pup will need two bowls, one for food and one for water. You may want two sets of bowls, one for inside and one for outside, depending on where the dog will be fed and where he will be spending most of his time. Stainless steel or sturdy plastic bowls are popular choices. Plastic bowls are more chewable. Dogs tend not to chew on the steel variety, which can be sterilised. It is important to buy sturdy bowls since anything is in danger of being chewed by puppy teeth and you do not want your dog to be constantly chewing apart his bowl (for his safety and for your purse!).

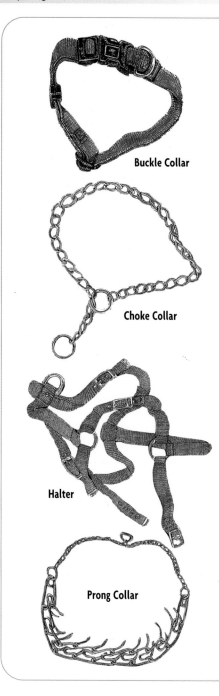

Buckle Collar

The BUCKLE COLLAR is the standard collar used for everyday purpose. Be sure that you adjust the buckle on growing puppies. Check it every day. It can become too tight overnight! These collars can be made of leather or nylon. Attach your dog's identification tags to this collar.

Choke Collar

The CHOKE CHAIN is the usual collar recommended for training. It is constructed of highly polished steel so that it slides easily through the stainless steel loop. The idea is that the dog controls the pressure around its neck and he will stop pulling if the collar becomes uncomfortable. Never leave a choke collar on your dog when not training.

Halter

The HALTER is for a trained dog that has to be restrained to prevent running away, chasing a cat and the like. Considered the most humane of all collars, it is frequently used on smaller dogs for which collars are not comfortable.

Prong Collar

The PRONG COLLAR certainly appears ominous, like an ancient instrument of torture. Although it is not intended to 'torture' a dog, it is only recommended on the most difficult of dogs, and *never* on small dogs. It should only be employed by someone who knows how to use it properly.

CLEANING SUPPLIES

Until a pup is housetrained you will be doing a lot of cleaning. Accidents will occur, which is okay in the beginning because the puppy does not know any better. All you can do is be prepared to clean up any 'accidents.' Old rags, towels, newspapers and a safe disinfectant are good to have on hand.

BEYOND THE BASICS

The items previously discussed are the bare necessities. You will find out what else you need as you go along—grooming supplies, flea/tick protection, etc. These things will vary depending on your situation but it is important that you have everything you need to feed and make your Shetland Sheepdog comfortable in his first few days at home.

PUPPY-PROOFING YOUR HOME

Aside from making sure that your Shetland Sheepdog will be comfortable in your home, you also have to make sure that your home is safe for your Shetland Sheepdog. This means taking precautions that your pup will not get into anything he should not get into and that there is nothing within his reach that may harm him should he sniff it, chew it, inspect it, etc. This probably seems obvious since, whilst you are primarily concerned with your pup's safety, at the same time you

Pet shops usually stock a large variety of water and food bowls for your dog.

Stainless steel or heavy plastic bowls are two of the most popular types for dogs.

Special equipment is available to make cleaning up a lot easier.

make a great chew toy? Cords should be fastened tightly against the wall. If your dog is going to spend time in a crate, make sure that there is nothing near his crate that he can reach if he sticks his curious little nose or paws through the openings. Just as you would with a child, keep all household clean-

do not want your belongings to be ruined. Breakables should be placed out of reach if your dog is to have full run of the house. If he is to be limited to certain places within the house, keep any potentially dangerous items in the 'off-limits' areas. An electrical cord can pose a danger should the puppy decide to taste it—and who is going to convince a pup that it would not

Financial Responsibility

Grooming tools, collars, leashes, dog beds and, of course, toys will be an expense to you when you first obtain your pup, and the cost will trickle on throughout your dog's lifetime. If your puppy damages or destroys your possessions (as most puppies surely will!) or something belonging to a neighbour, you can calculate additional expense. There is also flea and pest control, which every dog owner faces more than once. You must be able to handle the financial responsibility of owning a dog.

ers and chemicals where the pup cannot get to them.

It is also important to make sure that the outside of your home is safe. Of course your puppy should never be unsupervised, but a pup let loose in the garden will want to run and explore, and he

Puppies will play with anything. Take care that their toys are suitable. Suitable toys, made for puppies not children, cannot be swallowed and should not be so delicate they can be torn into small pieces.

should be granted that freedom. Do not let a fence give you a false sense of security; you would be surprised how crafty (and persistent) a dog can be in figuring out how to dig under and squeeze his way through small holes, or to jump or climb over a fence. The remedy is to make the fence high enough so that it really is impossible for your dog to get over it (about 3 metres should suffice),

Puppy-Proofing

Thoroughly puppy-proof your house before bringing your puppy home. Never use roach or rodent poisons in any area accessible to the puppy. Avoid the use of toilet bowl cleaners. Most dogs are born with toilet bowl sonar and will take a drink if the lid is left open. Also keep the trash secured and out of reach.

53

Shetland Sheepdog puppies live to play. Whether it's chasing a ball, fetching a flying disc or 'herding' their owner's children, puppies look forward to lots of daily fun.

and well embedded into the ground. Be sure to repair or secure any gaps in the fence. Check the fence periodically to ensure that it is in good shape and make repairs as needed; a very determined pup may return to the same spot to 'work on it' until he is able to get through.

FIRST TRIP TO THE VET
You have picked out your puppy, and your home and family are ready. Now all you have to do is collect your Shetland Sheepdog from the breeder and the fun begins, right? Well…not so fast. Something else you need to prepare is your pup's first trip to the veterinary surgeon. Perhaps the breeder can recommend someone in the area that specialises in Shetland Sheepdogs, or maybe you know some other Shetland Sheepdog owners who can suggest a good vet. Either way, you should have an appointment arranged for your pup before you pick him up and plan on taking him for an examination before bringing him home.

The pup's first visit will consist of an overall examination to make sure that the pup does not have any problems that are not apparent to the eye. The veterinary surgeon will also set up a schedule for the pup's vaccinations; the breeder will inform you of which ones the pup has already received and the vet can continue from there.

Toxic Plants

Many plants can be toxic to dogs. If you see your dog carrying a piece of vegetation in his mouth, approach him in a quiet, disinterested manner, avoid eye contact, pet him and gradually remove the plant from his mouth. Alternatively, offer him a treat and maybe he'll drop the plant on his own accord. Be sure no toxic plants are growing in your own garden.

Natural Toxins

Examine your lawn and garden landscaping before bringing your puppy home. Many varieties of plants have leaves, stems or flowers that are toxic if ingested, and you can depend on a curious puppy to investigate them. Ask your veterinarian for information on poisonous plants or research them at your library.

INTRODUCTION TO THE FAMILY

Everyone in the house will be excited about the puppy coming home and will want to pet him and play with him, but it is best to make the introduction low-key so as not to overwhelm the puppy. He is apprehensive already. It is the first time he has been separated from his mother and the breeder, and the ride to your home is likely the first time he has been in an auto. The last thing you want to do is smother him, as this will only frighten him further. This is not to say that human contact is not extremely necessary at this stage, because this is the time when a connection between the pup and his human family is formed. Gentle petting and soothing words should help console him, as well as just putting him down and letting him explore on his own (under your watchful eye, of course).

The pup may approach the family members or may busy himself with exploring for a while. Gradually, each person should spend some time with the pup, one at a time, crouching down to get as close to the pup's level as possible and letting him sniff their hands and petting him gently. He definitely needs human attention and he needs to be touched—this is how to form an immediate bond. Just remember that the pup is experiencing a lot of things for the first time, at the same time. There are new people, new noises, new smells, and new things to investigate: so be gentle, be affectionate, and be as comforting as you can be.

YOUR PUP'S FIRST NIGHT HOME

You have travelled home with your new charge safely in his basket or crate. He's been to the vet for a thorough check-over; he's been weighed, his papers examined; perhaps he's even been vac-

Chemical Toxins

Scour your carport for potential puppy dangers. Remove weed killers, pesticides and antifreeze materials. Antifreeze is highly toxic and even a few drops can kill an adult dog. The sweet taste attracts the animal, who will quickly consume it from the floor or curbside.

Each member of the household should spend some time with the new arrival, including the children. Since children tend to be excited about meeting the puppy, adults should supervise the proceedings.

Choose a cosy but safe place for the Sheltie puppy to stay in your home. Keep the pup away from anything that can cause him harm.

cinated and wormed as well. He's met the family, licked the whole family, including the excited children and the less-than-happy cat. He's explored his area, his new bed, the garden and anywhere else he's been permitted. He's eaten his first meal at home and relieved himself in the proper place. He's heard lots of new sounds, smelled new friends and seen more of the outside world than ever before.

That was just the first day! He's worn out and is ready for bed...or so you think!

It's puppy's first night and you are ready to say 'Good night'—keep in mind that this is puppy's first night ever to be sleeping alone. His dam and littermates are no longer at paw's length and he's a bit scared, cold and lonely. Be reassuring to your new family

member. This is not the time to spoil him and give in to his inevitable whining.

Puppies whine. They whine to let the others know where they are and hopefully to get company out of it. Place your pup in his new bed or crate in his room and close the door. Mercifully, he may fall asleep without a peep. If the inevitable occurs, ignore the whining: he is fine. Be strong and keep his interest in mind. Do not allow your heart to become guilty and visit the pup. He will fall asleep.

Many breeders recommend placing a piece of bedding from his former homestead in his new bed so that he recognises the scent of his littermates. Others still

advise placing a hot water bottle in his bed for warmth. This latter may be a good idea provided the pup doesn't attempt to suckle—he'll get good and wet and may not fall asleep so fast.

Puppy's first night can be somewhat stressful for the pup and his new family. Remember that you are setting the tone of nighttime at your house. Unless you want to play with your pup every evening at 10 p.m., midnight and 2 a.m., don't initiate the habit. Your family will thank you, and so will your pup!

PREVENTING PUPPY PROBLEMS

SOCIALISATION

Now that you have done all of the preparatory work and have helped your pup get accustomed to his new home and family, it is about time for you to have some fun! Socialising your Shetland Sheepdog pup gives you the opportunity to show off your new friend, and your pup gets to reap the benefits of being an adorable furry creature that people will want to pet and, in general, think is absolutely precious!

Besides getting to know his new family, your puppy should be exposed to other people, animals and situations, but of course he must not come into close contact with dogs you don't know well until his course of injections is fully complete. This will help him

become well adjusted as he grows up and less prone to being timid or fearful of the new things he will encounter. Your pup's socialisation began at the breeder's but now it is your responsibility to continue it. The socialisation he receives up until the age of 12

> **Did You Know?**
>
> Some experts in canine health advise that stress during a dog's early years of development can compromise and weaken his immune system and may trigger the potential for a shortened life expectancy. They emphasise the need for happy and stress-free growing-up years.

The move from his mother and litter-mates to your home is a big transition for a small pup, but your Sheltie will become part of the family in no time!

57

weeks is the most critical, as this is the time when he forms his impressions of the outside world. Be especially careful during the eight-to-ten-week period, also known as the fear period. The interaction he receives during this time should be gentle and reassuring. Lack of socialisation can manifest itself in fear and aggression as the dog grows up. He needs lots of human contact, affection, handling and exposure to other animals.

Once your pup has received his necessary vaccinations, feel free to take him out and about (on his lead, of course). Walk him around the neighbourhood, take him on your daily errands, let people pet him, let him meet other dogs and pets, etc. Puppies do not have to try to make friends; there will be no shortage of people who will want

Socialisation

Thorough socialisation includes not only meeting new people but also being introduced to new experiences such as riding in the auto, having his coat brushed, hearing the television, walking in a crowd—the list is endless. The more your pup experiences, and the more positive the experiences are, the less of a shock and the less scary it will be for your pup to encounter new things.

to introduce themselves. Just make sure that you carefully supervise each meeting. If the neighbourhood children want to say hello, for example, that is great—children and pups most often make great companions. Sometimes an excited child can unintentionally handle a pup too roughly, or an overzealous pup can playfully nip a little too hard. You want to make socialisation experiences positive ones. What a pup learns during this very formative stage will impact his attitude toward future encounters. You want your dog to be comfortable around everyone. A pup that has a bad experience with a child may grow up to be a dog that is shy around or aggressive toward children.

CONSISTENCY IN TRAINING

Dogs, being pack animals, naturally need a leader, or else they try to establish dominance in their packs. When you bring a dog into your family, the choice of who becomes the leader and who becomes the 'pack' is entirely up to you! Your pup's intuitive quest for dominance, coupled with the fact that it is nearly impossible to look at an adorable Shetland Sheepdog pup, with his 'puppy-dog' eyes and his too-big-for-his-head-still-floppy ears, and not cave in, give the pup almost an unfair advantage in getting the upper hand! A pup will definitely test the waters to see what he can and cannot do. Do not give in to those pleading eyes—stand your ground when it comes to disciplining the pup and make sure that all family members do the same. It will only confuse the pup when Mother tells him to get off the couch when he is used to sitting up there with Father to watch the nightly news. Avoid discrepancies by having all members of the household decide on the rules before the pup even comes home…and be consistent in enforcing them! Early training shapes the dog's personality, so you cannot be unclear in what you expect.

All puppies need a leader, and these Sheltie babies seem to be content in following around their young friend.

COMMON PUPPY PROBLEMS

The best way to prevent puppy problems is to be proactive in stopping an undesirable behaviour as soon as it starts. The old saying 'You can't teach an old dog new tricks' does not necessarily hold true, but it is true that it is much easier to discourage bad behaviour in a young developing pup than to wait until the pup's bad behaviour becomes the adult dog's bad habit. There are some problems that are especially prevalent in puppies as they develop.

NIPPING

Shelties need to learn to inhibit their bite reflex and never use their teeth on people, forbidden objects and other animals in play. Whenever you play with your puppy, you make the rules. This becomes an important message to your puppy in teaching him that you are the pack leader and control everything he does in life. Once your dog accepts you as his leader, you relationship with him is cemented for life! And in Shelties, the genetic factor for a permanent attachment to a master is so strong that he's literally born looking for a leader.

Nipping must be discouraged immediately and consistently with a firm 'No!' (or whatever number of firm 'No's' it takes for him to understand that you mean business). Then replace your finger with an appropriate chew toy. Whilst this behaviour is merely

59

Chewing Tips

Chewing goes hand in hand with nipping in the sense that a teething puppy is always looking for a way to soothe his aching gums. In this case, instead of chewing on you, he may have taken a liking to your favourite shoe or something else which he should not be chewing. Again, realise that this is a normal canine behaviour that does not need to be discouraged, only redirected. Your pup just needs to be taught what is acceptable to chew on and what is off limits. Consistently tell him NO when you catch him chewing on something forbidden and give him a chew toy. Conversely, praise him when you catch him chewing on something appropriate. In this way you are discouraging the inappropriate behaviour and reinforcing the desired behaviour. The puppy chewing should stop after his adult teeth have come in, but an adult dog continues to chew for various reasons—perhaps because he is bored, perhaps to relieve tension or perhaps he just likes to chew. That is why it is important to redirect his chewing when he is still young.

Your Sheltie should always feel comfortable in his crate. More than one dog means more than one crate, and crates should be of the proper size.

annoying when the dog is young, it can become dangerous as your Shetland Sheepdog's adult teeth grow in and his jaws develop, and he continues to think it is okay to gnaw on human appendages. Your Shetland Sheepdog does not mean any harm with a friendly nip, and his herding instincts and nipping may go paw in paw. Many herding dogs move their charges by nipping at their heels—your talented Sheltie may try this mechanism on the family cat, children or even you.

CRYING/WHINING

Your pup will often cry, whine, whimper, howl or make some type of commotion when he is left alone. This is basically his

way of calling out for attention to make sure that you know he is there and that you have not forgotten about him. He feels insecure when he is left alone, when you are out of the house and he is in his crate or when you are in another part of the house and he cannot see you. The noise he is making is an expression of the anxiety he feels at being alone, so he needs to be taught that being alone is okay. You are not actually training the dog to stop making noise, you are training him to feel comfortable when he is alone and thus removing the need for him to make the noise. This is where the crate filled with cosy bedding and a toy comes in handy. You want to know that he is safe when you are not there to supervise, and you know that he will be safe in his crate rather than roaming freely about the house. In order for the pup to stay in his crate without making a fuss, he needs to be comfortable in his crate. On that note, it is extremely important that the crate is never used as a form of punishment, or the pup will have a negative association with the crate.

Accustom the pup to the crate in short, gradually increasing time intervals in which you put him in the crate, maybe with a treat, and stay in the room with him. If he cries or makes a

Training Tip

Training your puppy takes much patience and can be frustrating at times, but you should see results from your efforts. If you have a puppy that seems untrainable, take him to a trainer or behaviourist. The dog may have a personality problem that requires the help of a professional, or perhaps you need help in learning how to train your dog.

fuss, do not go to him, but stay in his sight. Gradually he will realise that staying in his crate is all right without your help, and it will not be so traumatic for him when you are not around. You may want to leave the radio on softly when you leave the house; the sound of human voices may be comforting to him.

Did You Know?

You will probably start feeding your pup the same food that he has been getting from the breeder; the breeder should give you a few days' supply to start you off. Although you should not give your pup too many treats, you will want to have puppy treats on hand for coaxing, training, rewards, etc. Be careful, though, as a small pup's calorie requirements are relatively low and a few treats can add up to almost a full day's worth of calories without the required nutrition.

Internal Organs
with Skeletal Structure

1. Esophagus
2. Lungs
3. Gall Bladder
4. Liver
5. Kidney
6. Stomach
7. Intestines
8. Urinary Bladder

DIETARY AND FEEDING CONSIDERATIONS

Today the choices of food for your Shetland Sheepdog are many and varied. There are simply dozens of brands of food in all sorts of flavours and textures, ranging from puppy diets to those for seniors. There are even hypoallergenic and low-calorie diets available. Because your Sheltie's food has a bearing on coat, health and temperament, it is essential that the most suitable diet is selected for a Sheltie of his age. It is fair to say, however, that even dedicated owners can be somewhat perplexed by the enormous range of foods available. Only understanding what is best for your dog will help you reach a valued decision.

Dog foods are produced in three basic types: dried, semi-moist and tinned. Dried foods are useful for the cost-conscious for overall they tend to be less expensive than semi-moist or tinned. These contain the least fat and the most preservatives. In general tinned foods are made up of 60–70 percent water, whilst semi-moist ones often contain so much sugar that they are perhaps the least preferred by owners, even though their dogs seem to like them.

When selecting your dog's diet, three stages of development must be considered: the puppy stage, adult stage and the senior or veteran stage.

Food Preference

Selecting the best dried dog food is difficult. There is no majority consensus amongst veterinary scientists as to the value of nutrient analyses (protein, fat, fibre, moisture, ash, cholesterol, minerals, etc.). All agree that feeding trials are what matters, but you also have to consider the individual dog. Its weight, age, activity and what pleases its taste, all must be considered. It is probably best to take the advice of your veterinary surgeon. Every dog's dietary requirements vary, even during the lifetime of a particular dog.

If your dog is fed a good dried food, it does not require supplements of meat or vegetables. Dogs do appreciate a little variety in their diets so you may choose to stay with the same brand, but vary the flavour. Alternatively you may wish to add a little flavoured stock to give a difference to the taste.

PUPPY STAGE

Puppies instinctively want to suck milk from their mother's teats and a normal puppy will exhibit this behaviour from just a few moments following birth. If puppies do not attempt to suckle within the first half-hour or so, they should be encouraged to do so by placing them on the nipples, having selected ones with plenty of milk. This early

milk supply is important in providing colostrum to protect the puppies during the first eight to ten weeks of their lives. Although a mother's milk is much better than any milk formula, despite there being some excellent ones available, if the puppies do not feed you will have to feed them yourself. For those with less experience, advice from a veterinary surgeon is important so that you feed not only the right quantity of milk but that of correct quality, fed at suitably frequent intervals, usually every two hours during the first few days of life.

Puppies should be allowed to nurse from their mothers for about the first six weeks, although from the third or fourth week you will have begun to introduce small portions of suitable solid food. Most breeders like to introduce alternate milk and meat meals initially, building up to weaning time.

What are you feeding your dog?

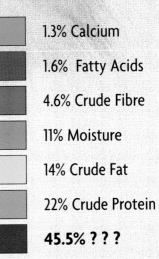

Read the label on your dog food. Many dog foods only advise what 50—55% of the contents are, leaving the other 45% to doubt.

1.3% Calcium

1.6% Fatty Acids

4.6% Crude Fibre

11% Moisture

14% Crude Fat

22% Crude Protein

45.5% ? ? ?

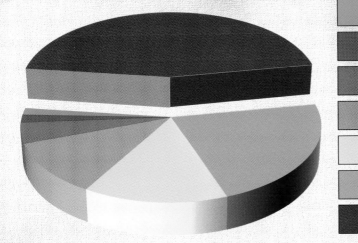

will have been reduced over time, only when a young dog has reached the age of about 18 months should an adult diet be fed.

Puppy and junior diets should be well balanced for the needs of your dog, so that except in certain circumstances additional vitamins, minerals and proteins will not be required.

ADULT DIETS

A dog is considered an adult when it has stopped growing, so in general the diet of a Sheltie can be changed to an adult one at about 10 to 12 months of age. Again you should rely upon your veterinary surgeon or dietary specialist to recommend an acceptable maintenance diet. Major dog food manufacturers specialise in this type of food, and it is just necessary for you to select the one best suited to your dog's needs. Active dogs may have different requirements than sedate dogs.

SENIOR DIETS

As dogs get older, their metabolism changes. The older dog usually exercises less, moves more slowly and sleeps more. This change in lifestyle and physiological performance requires a change in diet. Since these changes take place slowly, they might not be recognisable. What is easily recognisable is weight gain. By continuing to feed your dog an adult-

Puppy diets differ from adult diets. Discuss the diet of your puppy with the breeder. It is advisable to continue feeding the same brand food that the breeder offered. Any sudden change in the diet will upset the puppy's stomach.

By the time the puppies are seven or a maximum of eight weeks old, they should be fully weaned and fed solely on a proprietary puppy food. Selection of the most suitable, good-quality diet at this time is essential for a puppy's fastest growth rate is during the first year of life. Veterinary surgeons are usually able to offer advice in this regard and, although the frequency of meals

Did You Know?

You must store your dry dog food carefully. Open packages of dog food quickly lose their vitamin value, usually within 90 days of being opened. Mould spores and vermin could also contaminate the food.

maintenance diet when it is slowing down metabolically, your dog will gain weight. Obesity in an older dog compounds the health problems that already accompany old age.

As your dog gets older, few of his organs function up to par. The kidneys slow down and the intestines become less efficient. These age-related factors are best handled with a change in diet and a change in feeding schedule to give smaller portions that are more easily digested.

There is no single best diet for every older dog. Whilst many dogs do well on light or senior diets, other dogs do better on puppy diets or other special premium diets such as lamb and rice. Be sensitive to your senior Sheltie's diet and this will help control other problems that may arise with your old friend.

WATER

Just as your dog needs proper nutrition from his food, water is an essential 'nutrient' as well. Water keeps the dog's body properly hydrated and promotes normal function of the body's systems. During housebreaking it is necessary to keep an eye on how much water your Sheltie is drinking, but once he is reliably trained he should have access to clean fresh water at all times. Make sure that the dog's water bowl is clean, and change the water often, making sure that water is always available

for your dog, especially if you feed dried food.

EXERCISE

Although a Shetland Sheepdog is small, he is an active dog that requires ample exercise. A seden-

A balanced diet is absolutely essential, especially during your Sheltie's puppy's first year. This is the time when the puppy's growth rate is the fastest.

Grain-Based Diets

Many adult diets are based on grain. There is nothing wrong with this as long as it does not contain soy meal. Diets based on soy often cause flatulence (passing gas).

Grain-based diets are almost always the least expensive and a good grain diet is just as good as the most expensive diet containing animal protein.

There are many cases, however, when your dog might require a special diet. These special requirements should only be recommended by your veterinary surgeon.

Walking the Sheltie puppy on lead is the best form of daily exercise for both dog and owner. Begin lead training as soon as the puppy gets settled into your home.

exercise for the Sheltie. For those who are more ambitious, you will find that your Sheltie also enjoys long walks, an occasional hike or even a swim! Bear in mind that an overweight dog should never be suddenly over-exercised; instead he should be allowed to increase exercise slowly. Not only is exercise essential to keep the dog's body fit, it is essential to his mental well being. A bored dog will find something to do, which often manifests itself in some type of destructive behaviour. In this sense, it is essential for the owner's mental well-being as well!

Your Sheltie should be brushed every day in order to keep his coat from matting and knotting and to remove the loose hairs. You will need to teach the Sheltie to lay down on his side for part of the grooming ritual.

tary lifestyle is as harmful to a dog as it is to a person. The Sheltie is a fairly active breed that enjoys exercise, but you don't have to be an Olympic athlete! Regular walks, play sessions in the garden, or letting the dog run free in the garden under your supervision are sufficient forms of

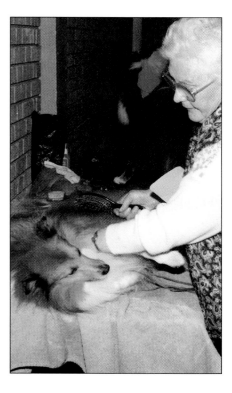

Did You Know?

The use of human soap products like shampoo, bubble bath and hand soap can be damaging to a dog's coat and skin. Human products are too strong and remove the protective oils coating the dog's hair and skin (making him water-resistant). Use only shampoo made especially for dogs and you may like to use a medicated shampoo, which will always help to keep external parasites at bay.

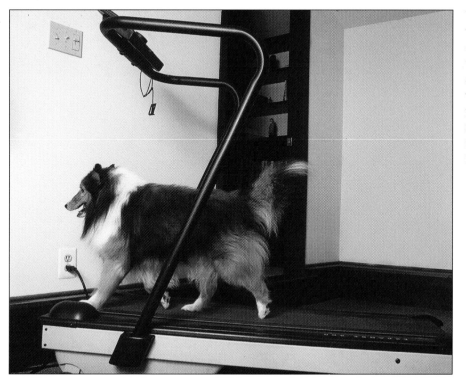

There are no limitations to the kinds of exercise your Sheltie will welcome. If you are fortunate enough to have a treadmill, you can train your Sheltie to use it. This is especially useful in inclement weather.

GROOMING

BRUSHING

A metal comb and a natural bristle brush designed for use on long coats are necessities for grooming Shelties. A pet supply store will be able to suggest the appropriate items for use on Shelties so be sure to explain to the shopkeeper for which breed of dog you are shopping for supplies.

Everyday care of the Sheltie means that you will be brushing him daily. Daily brushing is effective for removing dead hair and stimulating the dog's natural oils to add shine and a healthy look to the coat. If you brush your Sheltie regularly, he will not get matted, therefore the brushing will take only minutes because there are not matts with which to contend. If taught to stand still or lie down for a short daily brushing session, Shelties come to love grooming time and look forward to a biscuit when the process is completed. Regular grooming sessions are also a good way to spend time with your dog.

BATHING

Dogs do not need to be bathed as often as humans, but regular bathing is essential for healthy

69

This is the proper way to carry and lift a Sheltie. He is being taken to his bath and he looks a bit hesitant! Talk soothingly to the dog to comfort him if he resists the idea of bathing.

Rinse the dog thoroughly before applying the dog shampoo. Be sure to keep the dog's head and ears from the spray of the nozzle.

skin and a healthy, shiny coat. Again, like most anything, if you accustom your pup to being bathed as a puppy, it will be second nature by the time he grows up. You want your dog to be at ease in the bath or else it could end up a wet, soapy, messy ordeal for both of you!

Brush your Sheltie thoroughly before wetting his coat. This will get rid of most mats and tangles, which are harder to remove when the coat is wet. Make that your dog has a good non-slip surface to stand on. Begin by wetting the dog's coat. A shower or hose attachment is necessary for thor-

70

oughly wetting and rinsing the coat. Check the water temperature to make sure that it is neither too hot nor too cold.

Next, apply shampoo to the dog's coat and work it into a good lather. You should purchase a shampoo that is made for dogs. Do not use a product made for human

hair. Wash the head last; you do not want shampoo to drip into the dog's eyes whilst you are washing the rest of his body. Work the shampoo all the way down to the skin. You can use this opportunity to check the skin for any bumps, bites or other abnormalities. Do not neglect any area of the body—get all of the hard-to-reach places.

Once the dog has been thoroughly shampooed, he requires an equally thorough rinsing. Shampoo left in the coat can be irritating to the skin. Protect his eyes from the shampoo by shielding them with your hand and directing the flow of water in the opposite direction. You should also avoid getting water in the ear

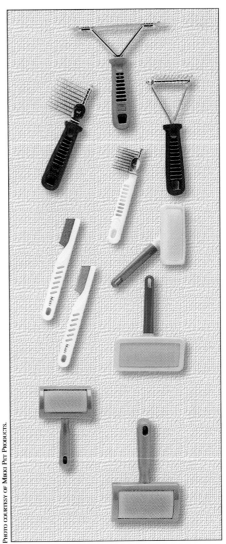

PHOTO COURTESY OF MIKKI PET PRODUCTS.

Towel dry the dog as swiftly as possible. Every dog shakes out his coat when wet. By immediately wrapping him in a towel, you will remove most of the water before he gives you your 'shower.'

Your local pet shop will be able to offer you suitable grooming tools, especially brushes and rakes made for long-haired breeds.

canal. Be prepared for your dog to shake out his coat—you might want to stand back, but make sure you have a hold on the dog to keep him from running through the house.

71

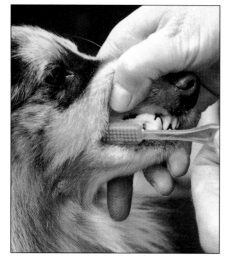

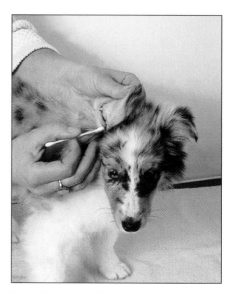

Cleaning your dog's teeth is also a part of the grooming process. Ask your vet about proper maintenance of your dog's teeth. Whilst brushing can be done at home, scraping is usually done at the vet's office.

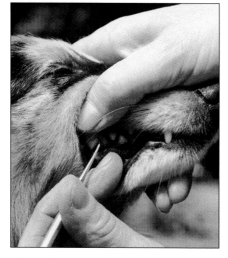

Your Sheltie's ears should be cleaned and examined for mites.

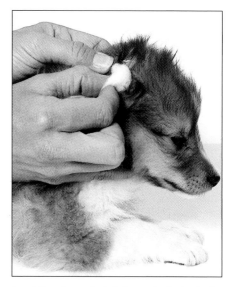

EAR CLEANING

The ears should be kept clean and any excess hair inside the ear should be carefully removed. Ears can be cleaned with special cotton wipes made for dogs. Be on the lookout for any signs of infection or ear mite infestation. If your

A specially made ear wipe is the best option for cleaning the Sheltie's ears. The outside of the ear should also be thoroughly examined and cleaned.

Nail Clipping

Quick

Cut Line

Nail Casing

DARK-COLOURED NAIL

With black or dark nails, it's best to clip only a small bit of the nail at a time or to use a file where the quick is not visible.

LIGHT-COLOURED NAIL

In light-coloured nails, clipping is much simpler because you can see the vein (or quick) that grows inside the casing.

Carefully clean the area around your Sheltie's eyes with a soft wipe and special cleaner.

Sheltie has been shaking his head or scratching at his ears frequently, this usually indicates a problem. If his ears have an unusual odour, this is a sure sign of mite infestation or infection, and a signal to have his ears checked by the veterinary surgeon.

NAIL CLIPPING

Your Sheltie should be accustomed to having his nails trimmed at an early age, since it will be part of your maintenance routine throughout his life. Not only does it look nicer, but long nails can be sharp if they scratch someone unintentionally. Also, a long nail has a better chance of ripping and bleeding, or causing the feet to spread. A good rule of thumb is that if you can hear your dog's nails clicking on the floor when he walks, his nails are too long.

Before you start cutting, make sure you can identify the 'quick' in each nail. The quick is a blood

Your dog's nails should be trimmed regularly. Dogs that run on hard surfaces usually wear their nails down and don't require clipping as often as dogs who are mostly on grass.

Opposite page: Typical hairs enlarged hundreds of times their natural size. The cuticle (outer covering) is very clean. The inset shows the growing tip. S.E.M. by Dr Dennis Kunkel, University of Hawaii.

vessel that runs through the centre of each nail and grows rather close to the end. It will bleed if accidentally cut, which will be quite painful for the dog as it contains nerve endings. Keep some type of clotting agent on hand, such as a styptic pencil or styptic powder (the type used for shaving). This will stop the bleeding quickly when applied to the end of the cut nail. Do not panic if this happens, just stop the bleeding and talk soothingly to your dog. Once he has calmed down, move on to the next nail. It is better to clip a little at a time, particularly with black-nailed dogs.

Hold your pup steady as you begin trimming his nails; you do not want him to make any sudden movements or run away. Talk to him soothingly and stroke him as you clip. Holding his foot in your hand, simply take off the end of each nail in one quick clip. You can purchase nail clippers that are specially made for dogs; you can probably find them wherever you buy pet or grooming supplies.

TRAVELLING WITH YOUR DOG
CAR TRAVEL

You should accustom your Sheltie to riding in a car at an early age. You may or may not take him in the car often, but at the very least he will need to go to the vet and you do not want these trips to be traumatic for the dog or a big hassle for you. The safest way for a dog to ride in the car is in his crate. If he uses a crate in the house, you can use the same crate for travel.

Put the pup in the crate and see how he reacts. If he seems uneasy, you can have a passenger hold him on his lap whilst you drive. Another option is a special-

Grooming Equipment

How much grooming equipment you purchase will depend on how much grooming you are going to do. Here are some basics:

• Natural bristle brush
• Slicker brush
• Metal comb
• Scissors
• Blaster
• Rubber mat
• Dog shampoo
• Spray hose attachment
• Ear cleaner
• Cotton wipes
• Towels
• Nail clippers

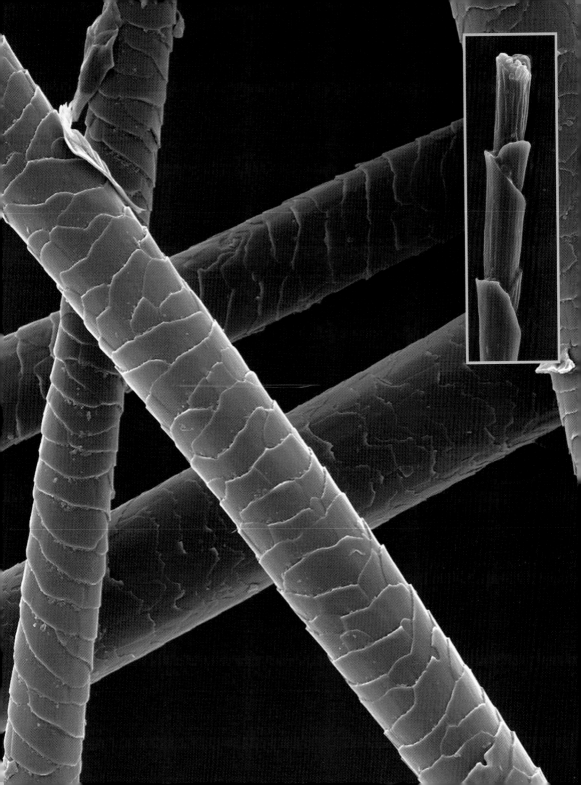

ly made safety harness for dogs, which straps the dog in much like a seat belt. Do not let the dog roam loose in the vehicle—this is very dangerous! If you should stop short, your dog can be thrown and injured. If the dog starts climbing on you and pestering you whilst you are driving, you will not be able to concentrate on the road. It is an unsafe situation for everyone—human and canine.

For long trips, be prepared to stop to let the dog relieve himself. Bring along whatever you need to clean up after him. You should take along some paper kitchen towels and perhaps some old towelling for use should he have an accident in the car or suffer from travel sickness.

Did You Know?

A dog that spends a lot of time outside on a hard surface, such as cement or pavement, will have his nails naturally worn down and may not need to have them trimmed as often, except maybe in the colder months when he is not outside as much. Regardless, it is best to get your dog accustomed to this procedure at an early age so that he is used to it. Some dogs are especially sensitive about having their feet touched, but if a dog has experienced it since he was young, he should not be bothered by it.

AIR TRAVEL

Whilst it is possible to take a dog on a flight within Britain, this is fairly unusual and advance permission is always required. The dog will be required to travel in a fibreglass crate and you should always check in advance with the airline regarding specific requirements. To help the dog be at ease, put one of his favourite toys in the crate with him. Do not feed the dog for at least six hours before the trip to minimise his need to relieve himself. However, certain regulations specify that water must always be made available to the dog in the crate.

Make sure your dog is properly identified and that your contact information appears on his ID tags

him to a neighbour's house to stay whilst you are gone, to have a trusted neighbour stop by often or stay at your house, or bring your dog to a reputable boarding kennel. If you choose to board him at a kennel, you should visit in advance to see the facility, how clean they are and where the dogs are kept. Talk to some of the

Should you find it necessary to board your Sheltie, look for a kennel that is close by, clean, and spacious with ample exercise opportunities for your dog. Your vet can usually give you good advice about a suitable kennel for boarding.

and on his crate. Animals travel in a different area of the plane than human passengers so every rule must be strictly adhered to so as to prevent the risk of getting separated from your dog.

BOARDING

So you want to take a family holiday—and you want to include all members of the family. You would probably make arrangements for accommodations ahead of time anyway, but this is especially important when travelling with a dog. You do not want to make an overnight stop at the only place around for miles and find out that they do not allow dogs. Also, you do not want to reserve a place for your family without confirming that you are travelling with a dog because if it is against their policy you may not have a place to stay.

Alternatively, if you are travelling and choose not to bring your Sheltie, you will have to make arrangements for him whilst you are away. Some options are to take

employees and see how they treat the dogs—do they spend time with the dogs, play with them, exercise them, etc.? Also find out the kennel's policy on vaccinations and what they require. This is for all of the dogs' safety, since when dogs are kept together, there is a greater risk of diseases being passed from dog to dog.

IDENTIFICATION
Your Sheltie is your valued companion and friend. That is why you always keep a close eye on him and you have made sure that he cannot escape from the garden or wriggle out of his collar and run away from you. However, accidents can happen and there may come a time when your dog unexpectedly gets separated from you. If this unfortunate event should occur, the first thing on your mind will be finding him. Proper identification, including an ID tag, a tattoo, and possibly a microchip, will increase the chances of his being returned to you safely and quickly.

Identification

If your dog gets lost, he is not able to ask for directions home.

Identification tags fastened to the collar give important information—the dog's name, the owner's name, the owner's address and a telephone number where the owner can be reached. This makes it easy for whomever finds the dog to contact the owner and arrange to have the dog returned. An added advantage is that a person will be more likely to approach a lost dog who has ID tags on his collar; it tells the person that this is somebody's pet rather than a stray. This is the easiest and fastest method of identification provided that the tags stay on the collar and the collar stays on the dog.

Travel Tip

For international travel you will have to make arrangements well in advance (perhaps months), as countries' regulations pertaining to bringing in animals differ. There may be special health certificates and/or vaccinations that your dog will need before taking the trip, sometimes this has to be done within a certain time frame. In rabies-free countries, you will need to bring proof of the dog's rabies vaccination and there may be a quarantine period upon arrival.

Protect Your Pup

As puppies become more and more expensive, especially those puppies of high quality for showing and/or breeding, they have a greater chance of being stolen. The usual collar dog tag is, of course, easily removed. But there are two techniques that have become widely utilised for identification.

The puppy microchip implantation involves the injection of a small microchip, about the size of a corn kernel, under the skin of the dog. If your dog shows up at a clinic or shelter, or is offered for resale under less than savory circumstances, it can be positively identified by the microchip. The microchip is scanned and a registry quickly identifies you as the owner. This is not only protection against theft, but should the dog run away or go chasing a squirrel and get lost, you have a fair chance of getting it back.

Tattooing is done on various parts of the dog, from its belly to its cheeks. The number tattooed can be your telephone number or any other number which you can easily memorise. When professional dog thieves see a tattooed dog, they usually lose interest in it. Both microchipping and tattooing can be done at your local veterinary clinic. For the safety of our dogs, no laboratory facility or dog broker will accept a tattooed dog as stock.

Tattoos have become a very common method of permanently identifying a dog. With a breed as long-haired as the Sheltie, the ear is the location that is frequently chosen.

Your Shetland Sheepdog puppy has great value to you and should be protected, kept in a secure area and properly identified.

79

Training a single Sheltie is certainly more manageable than a half dozen! These six well-trained dogs walk nicely by their mistress's side.

Living with an untrained dog is a lot like owning a piano that you do not know how to play—it is a nice object to look at but it does not do much more than that to bring you pleasure. Now try taking piano lessons and suddenly the piano comes alive and brings forth magical sounds and rhythms that set your heart singing and your body swaying.

The same is true with your Shetland Sheepdog. Any dog is a big responsibility and if not trained sensibly may develop unacceptable behaviour that annoys you or could even cause family friction.

To train your Shetland Sheepdog, you may like to enrol in an obedience class. Teach him good manners as you learn how and why he behaves the

way he does. Find out how to communicate with your dog and how to recognise and understand his communications with you. Suddenly the dog takes on a new role in your life—he is smart, interesting, well behaved and fun to be with. He demonstrates his bond of devotion to you daily. In other words, your Shetland Sheepdog does wonders for your ego because he constantly reminds you that you are not only his leader, you are his hero!

Those involved with teaching dog obedience and counselling owners about their dogs' behaviour have discovered some interesting facts about dog ownership. For example, training dogs when

Did You Know?

Dogs are the most honourable animals in existence. They consider another species (humans) as their own. They interface with you. You are their leader. Puppies perceive children to be on their level; their actions around small children are different than their behaviour around their adult masters.

Shelties should be trained as early as possible. Even though they are trainable throughout their lives, the best and fastest results come from training in puppyhood.

they are puppies results in the highest rate of success in developing well-mannered and well-adjusted adult dogs. Training an older dog, from six months to six years of age, can produce almost equal results providing that the owner accepts the dog's slower rate of learning capability and is willing to work patiently to help the dog succeed at developing to his fullest potential. Unfortunately, many owners of untrained adult dogs lack the patience factor, so they do not persist until their dogs are successful at learning particular behaviours.

Training a puppy aged 10 to 16 weeks (20 weeks at the most) is like working with a dry sponge in a pool of water. The pup soaks up whatever you show him and constantly looks for more things to do and learn. At this early age, his body is not yet producing hormones, and therein lies the reason for such a high rate of success. Without hormones, he is focused on his owners and not particular-

Think Before YOU Bark!

Dogs are sensitive to their master's moods and emotions. Use your voice wisely when communicating with your dog. Never raise your voice at your dog unless you are angry and trying to correct him. 'Barking' at your dog can become as meaningless as 'dogspeak' is to you. Think before you bark!

Young puppies are better students than adolescent puppies. As soon as a dog's hormones start flowing, he is easily distracted and has other interests in life.

ly interested in investigating other places, dogs, people, etc. You are his leader: his provider of food, water, shelter and security. He latches onto you and wants to stay close. He will usually follow you from room to room, will not let you out of his sight when you are outdoors with him, and respond in like manner to the people and animals you encounter. If you greet a friend warmly, he will be happy to greet the person as well. If, however, you are hesitant, even anxious, about the approach of a stranger, he will respond accordingly.

Once the puppy begins to produce hormones, his natural curiosity emerges and he begins to investigate the world around him. It is at this time when you may notice that the untrained dog begins to wander away from you and even ignore your commands

to stay close. When this behaviour becomes a problem, the owner has two choices: get rid of the dog or train him. It is strongly urged that you choose the latter option.

There are usually classes within a reasonable distance from the owner's home, but you also can do a lot to train your dog yourself. Sometimes there are classes available but the tuition is too costly. Whatever the circumstances, the solution to the problem of lack of lesson availability lies within the pages of this book.

This chapter is devoted to helping you train your Shetland Sheepdog at home. If the recommended procedures are followed faithfully, you may expect positive results that will prove rewarding to both you and your dog.

Whether your new charge is a puppy or a mature adult, the methods of teaching and the techniques we use in training basic behaviours are the same. After all, no dog, whether puppy or adult, likes harsh or inhumane methods. All creatures, however, respond favourably to gentle motivational methods and sincere praise and encouragement. Now let us get started.

HOUSEBREAKING
You can train a puppy to relieve itself wherever you choose, but this must be somewhere suitable. You should bear in mind from the outset that when your puppy is old enough to go out in public places, any canine deposits must be removed at once. You will always have to carry with you a small plastic bag or 'poop-scoop.'

Outdoor training includes such surfaces as grass, dirt and cement. Indoor training usually means training your dog to newspaper.

When deciding on the surface and location that you will want

Mealtime

Mealtime should be a peaceful time for your puppy. Do not put his food and water bowls in a high-traffic area in the house. For example, give him his own little corner of the kitchen where he can eat undisturbed and where he will not be under foot. Do not allow small children or other family members to disrupt the pup when he is eating.

your Shetland Sheepdog to use, be sure it is going to be permanent. Training your dog to grass and then changing your mind two months later is extremely difficult for both dog and owner.

Next, choose the command you will use each and every time you want your puppy to void. 'Go hurry up' and 'Toilet' are examples of commands commonly used by dog owners.

Get in the habit of giving the puppy your chosen relief command before you take him out. That way, when he becomes an adult, you will be able to determine if he wants to go out when you ask him. A confirmation will be signs of interest, wagging his tail, watching you intently, going to the door, etc.

PUPPY'S NEEDS
Puppy needs to relieve himself after play periods, after each meal,

How Many Times a Day?

AGE	RELIEF TRIPS
To 14 weeks	10
14–22 weeks	8
22–32 weeks	6
Adulthood	4
(dog stops growing)	

These are estimates, of course, but they are a guide to the MINIMUM opportunities a dog should have each day to relieve itself.

83

ately after sleeping and eating. The older the puppy, the less often he will need to relieve himself. Finally, as a mature healthy adult, he will require only three to five relief trips per day.

HOUSING

Since the types of housing and control you provide for your puppy has a direct relationship on the success of housetraining, we consider the various aspects of both before we begin training.

Bringing a new puppy home and turning him loose in your house can be compared to turning a child loose in a sports arena and telling the child that the place is all his! The sheer enormity of the place would be too much for him to handle.

Instead, offer the puppy clearly defined areas where he can play, sleep, eat and live. A room of the house where the family gathers is the most obvious

after he has been sleeping and any time he indicates that he is looking for a place to urinate or defecate.

The urinary and intestinal tract muscles of very young puppies are not fully developed. Therefore, like human babies, puppies need to relieve themselves frequently.

Take your puppy out often—every hour for an eight-week-old, for example, and always immedi-

Your Sheltie pup begins socialisation with his littermates and continues with his new owners. This is an essential part of early training.

Training must be reinforced throughout the Sheltie's life. Practising commands should be a part of your dog's everyday life.

choice. Puppies are social animals and need to feel a part of the pack right from the start. Hearing your voice, watching you whilst you are doing things and smelling you nearby are all positive reinforcers that he is now a member of your pack. Usually a family room, the kitchen or a nearby adjoining breakfast area is ideal for providing safety and security for both puppy and owner.

Within that room there should be a smaller area which the puppy can call his own. An alcove, a wire or fibreglass dog crate or a fenced (not boarded!) corner from which he can view the activities of his new family will be fine. The size of the area or crate is the key factor here. The area must be large enough for the puppy to lie down and stretch out as well as stand up without rubbing his head on the top, yet small enough so that he cannot relieve himself at one end and sleep at the other without coming into contact with his droppings until fully trained to relieve himself outside.

Dogs are, by nature, clean animals and will not remain close to their relief areas unless forced to do so. In those cases, they then become

The Golden Rule

The golden rule of dog training is simple. For each 'question' (command), there is only one correct answer (reaction). One command = one reaction. Keep practising the command until the dog reacts correctly without hesitating. Be repetitive but not monotonous. Dogs get bored just as people do!

Did You Know?

To a dog's way of thinking, your hands are like his mouth in terms of a defence mechanism. If you squeeze him too tightly, he might just bite you because that would be his normal response. This is not aggressive biting and, although all biting should be discouraged, you need the discipline in learning how to handle your dog.

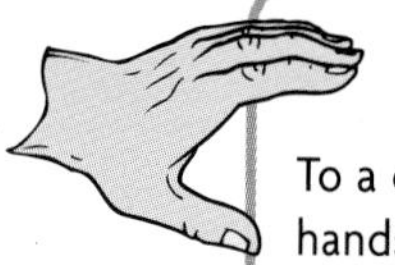

dirty dogs and usually remain that way for life.

The designated area should be lined with clean bedding and a toy. Water must always be available, in a non-spill container.

Control

By control, we mean helping the puppy to create a lifestyle pattern that will be compatible to that of his human pack (YOU!). Just as we guide little children to learn our way of life, we must show the puppy when it is time to play, eat, sleep, exercise and even entertain himself.

Your puppy should always sleep in his crate. He should also learn that, during times of household confusion and excessive human activity such as at breakfast when family members are preparing for the day, he can play by himself in relative safety and comfort in his designated area. Each time you leave the puppy alone, he should understand exactly where he is to stay. Puppies are chewers. They cannot tell the difference between lamp cords, television wires, shoes, table legs, etc. Chewing into a television wire, for example, can be fatal to the puppy whilst a shorted wire can start a fire in the house.

If the puppy chews on the arm of the chair when he is alone, you will probably discipline him angrily when you get home. Thus, he makes the association that your coming home means he is going to be punished. (He will not remember chewing up the chair and is incapable of making the association of the discipline with his naughty deed.)

Other times of excitement,

Housebreaking Tip

Most of all, be consistent. Always take your dog to the same location, always use the same command, and always have him on lead when he is in his relief area, unless a fenced-in garden is available.

By following the Success Method, your puppy will be completely housetrained by the time his muscle and brain development reach maturity. Keep in mind that small breeds usually mature faster than large breeds, but all puppies should be trained by six months of age.

such as family parties, etc., can be fun for the puppy providing he can view the activities from the security of his designated area. He is not underfoot and he is not being fed all sorts of titbits that will probably cause him stomach distress, yet he still feels a part of the fun.

SCHEDULE

A puppy should be taken to his relief area each time he is released from his designated area, after meals, after a play session, when he first awakens in the morning (at age eight weeks, this can mean 5 a.m.!). The puppy will indicate that he's ready 'to go' by circling or sniffing busily—-do not misinterpret these signs. For a puppy less than ten weeks of age, a routine of taking him out every hour is necessary. As the puppy grows, he will be able to wait for longer periods of time.

Keep trips to his relief area short. Stay no more than five or six minutes and then return to the

Did You Know?

By providing sleeping and resting quarters that fit the dog, and offering frequent opportunities to relieve himself outside his quarters, the puppy quickly learns that the outdoors (or the newspaper if you are training him to paper) is the place to go when he needs to urinate or defecate. It also reinforces his innate desire to keep his sleeping quarters clean. This, in turn, helps develop the muscle control that will eventually produce a dog with clean living habits.

Grass is the most common relief surface on which to train a puppy. When not in your own garden, be sure to clean up after the dog immediately.

Housebreaking Tip

Do not carry your dog to his toilet area. Lead him there on a leash or, better yet, encourage him to follow you to the spot. If you start carrying him to his spot, you might end up doing this routine forever and your dog will have the satisfaction of having trained YOU.

house. If he goes during that time, praise him lavishly and take him indoors immediately. If he does not, but he has an accident when you go back indoors, pick him up immediately, say 'No! No!' and return to his relief area. Wait a few minutes, then return to the house again. never hit a puppy or rub his face in urine or excrement

87

when he has an accident!

Once indoors, put the puppy in his crate until you have had time to clean up his accident. Then release him to the family area and watch him more closely than before. Chances are, his accident was a result of your not picking up his signal or waiting too long before offering him the opportunity to relieve himself. Never hold a grudge against the puppy for accidents.

Let the puppy learn that going outdoors means it is time to relieve himself, not play. Once trained, he will be able to play indoors and out and still differentiate between the times for play versus the times for relief.

Help him develop regular hours for naps, being alone, playing by himself and just resting, all in his crate. Encourage him to entertain himself whilst you are busy with your activities. Let him learn that having you

near is comforting, but it is not your main purpose in life to provide him with undivided attention.

Each time you put a puppy in his own area, use the same command, whatever suits best. Soon, he will run to his crate or special area when he hears you say those words.

Crate training provides safety for you, the puppy and the home. It also provides the puppy with a feeling of security, and that helps the puppy achieve self-confidence and clean habits.

Remember that one of the primary ingredients in housetraining your puppy is control. Regardless of your lifestyle, there will always be occasions when you will need to have a place where your dog can stay and be happy and safe. Training is the answer for now and in the future.

In conclusion, a few key elements are really all you need for a successful house training method—consistency, frequency, praise, control and supervision. By following these procedures with a normal, healthy puppy, you and the puppy will soon be past the stage of 'accidents' and ready to move on to a full and rewarding life together.

ROLES OF DISCIPLINE, REWARD AND PUNISHMENT

Discipline, training one to act in accordance with rules, brings order to life. It is as simple as that. Without discipline, particularly in a group society, chaos reigns supreme and the group will eventually perish. Humans and canines are social animals and need some form of discipline in order to function effectively. They must procure food, protect their home base and their young and reproduce to keep the species going.

If there were no discipline in the lives of social animals, they would eventually die from starvation and/or predation by other stronger animals.

In the case of domestic canines, dogs need discipline in their lives in order to understand how their pack (you and other family members) functions and how they must act in order to survive.

A large humane society in a highly populated area recently surveyed dog owners regarding their satisfaction with their relationships with their dogs. People who had trained their dogs were 75% more satisfied with their pets than those who had never trained their dogs.

Dr Edward Thorndike, a psychologist, established *Thorndike's Theory of Learning*, which states

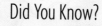

Did You Know?

Never line your pup's sleeping area with newspaper. Puppy litters are usually raised on newspaper and, once in your home, the puppy will immediately associate newspaper with voiding. Never put newspaper on any floor while housetraining, as this will only confuse the puppy. If you are paper-training him, use paper in his designated relief area ONLY. Finally, restrict water intake after evening meals. Offer a few licks at a time—never let a young puppy gulp water after meals.

that a behaviour that results in a pleasant event tends to be repeated. A behaviour that results in an unpleasant event tends not to be repeated. It is this theory on which training methods are based today. For example, if you manipulate a dog to perform a specific behaviour and reward him for doing it, he is likely to do it again because he enjoyed the end result.

Occasionally, punishment, a penalty inflicted for an offence, is necessary. The best type of punishment often comes from an outside source. For example, a child

THE SUCCESS METHOD
Steps to Successful Crate Training

1 Tell the puppy 'Crate time!' and place him in the crate with a small treat (a piece of cheese or half of a biscuit). Let him stay in the crate for five minutes while you are in the same room. Then release him and praise lavishly. Never release him when he is fussing. Wait until he is quiet before you let him out.

2 Repeat Step 1 several times a day.

3 The next day, place the puppy in the crate as before. Let him stay there for ten minutes. Do this several times.

4 Continue building time in five-minute increments until the puppy

stays in his crate for 30 minutes with you in the room. Always take him to his relief area after prolonged periods in his crate.

5 Now go back to Step 1 and let the puppy stay in his crate for five minutes, this time while you are out of the room.

6 Once again, build crate time in five-minute increments with you out of the room. When the puppy will stay willingly in his crate (he may even fall asleep!) for 30 minutes with you out of the room, he will be ready to stay in it for several hours at a time.

Canine Development Schedule

It is important to understand how and at what age a puppy develops into adulthood. If you are a puppy owner, consult the following Canine Development Schedule to determine the stage of development your puppy is currently experiencing. This knowledge will help you as you work with the puppy in the weeks and months ahead.

Period	Age	Characteristics
FIRST TO THIRD	**BIRTH TO SEVEN WEEKS**	Puppy needs food, sleep and warmth, and responds to simple and gentle touching. Needs mother for security and disciplining. Needs littermates for learning and interacting with other dogs. Pup learns to function within a pack and learns pack order of dominance. Begin socialising with adults and children for short periods. Begins to become aware of its environment.
FOURTH	**EIGHT TO TWELVE WEEKS**	Brain is fully developed. Needs socialising with outside world. Remove from mother and littermates. Needs to change from canine pack to human pack. Human dominance necessary. Fear period occurs between 8 and 16 weeks. Avoid fright and pain.
FIFTH	**THIRTEEN TO SIXTEEN WEEKS**	Training and formal obedience should begin. Less association with other dogs, more with people, places, situations. Period will pass easily if you remember this is pup's change-to-adolescence time. Be firm and fair. Flight instinct prominent. Permissiveness and over-disciplining can do permanent damage. Praise for good behaviour.
JUVENILE	**FOUR TO EIGHT MONTHS**	Another fear period about 7 to 8 months of age. It passes quickly, but be cautious of fright and pain. Sexual maturity reached. Dominant traits established. Dog should understand sit, down, come and stay by now.

NOTE: THESE ARE APPROXIMATE TIME FRAMES. ALLOW FOR INDIVIDUAL DIFFERENCES IN PUPPIES.

Practice Makes Perfect!

• Have training lessons with your dog every day in several short segments—three to five times a day for a few minutes at a time is ideal.

• Do not have long practice sessions. The dog will become easily bored.

• Never practice when you are tired, ill, worried or in an otherwise negative mood. This will transmit to the dog and may have an adverse effect on its performance.

Think fun, short and above all POSITIVE! End each session on a high note, rather than a failed exercise, and make sure to give a lot of praise. Enjoy the training and help your dog enjoy it, too.

TRAINING EQUIPMENT
COLLAR AND LEAD

For a Shetland Sheepdog the collar and lead that you use for training must be one with which you are easily able to work, not too heavy for the dog and perfectly safe.

TREATS

Have a bag of treats on hand. Something nutritious and easy to swallow works best. Use a soft treat, a chunk of cheese or a piece of cooked chicken rather than a dry biscuit. By the time the dog gets done chewing a dry treat, he

is told not to touch the stove because he may get burned. He disobeys and touches the stove. In doing so, he receives a burn. From that time on, he respects the heat of the stove and avoids contact with it. Therefore, a behaviour that results in an unpleasant event tends not to be repeated.

A good example of a dog learning the hard way is the dog who chases the house cat. He is told many times to leave the cat alone, yet he persists in teasing the cat. Then, one day he begins chasing the cat but the cat turns and swipes a claw across the dog's face, leaving him with a painful gash on his nose. The final result is that the dog stops chasing the cat.

will forget why he is being rewarded in the first place! Using food rewards will not teach a dog to beg at the table—the only way to teach a dog to beg at the table is to give him food from the table. In training, rewarding the dog with a food treat will help him associate praise and the treats with learning new behaviours that obviously please his owner.

TRAINING BEGINS: ASK THE DOG A QUESTION

In order to teach your dog anything, you must first get his attention. After all, he cannot learn

anything if he is looking away from you with his mind on something else.

To get his attention, ask him, 'School?' and immediately walk over to him and give him a treat as you tell him 'Good dog.' Wait a minute or two and repeat the routine, this time with a treat in your hand as you approach within a foot of the dog. Do not go directly to him, but stop about a foot short of him and hold out the treat as you ask, 'School?' He will see you approaching with a treat in your hand and most likely begin walking toward you. As you meet, give him the treat and praise again.

The third time, ask the question, have a treat in your hand and walk only a short distance toward the dog so that he must walk almost all the way to you. As he reaches you, give him the treat and praise again.

By this time, the dog will probably be getting the idea that if he pays attention to you, especially when you ask that question, it will pay off in treats and fun activities for him. In other words, he learns that 'school' means doing fun things with you that result in treats and positive attention for him.

Remember that the dog does not understand your verbal language, he only recognises sounds. Your question translates to a series of sounds for him, and those sounds become the signal to

Don't be afraid to motivate your puppy with treats. When initiating a training routine, use the lead to keep the puppy close and attentive.

Food rewards make training much easier. Most dogs are motivated by the smell of a tasty treat, so owners can use this to their advantage. Fortunately, Shelties are eager to please and enjoy learning.

your food hand from in front of the dog's nose up over his head so that he is looking at the ceiling. As he bends his head upward, he will have to bend his knees to maintain his balance. As he bends his knees, he will assume a sit position. At that point, release the food treat and praise lavishly with comments such as 'Good dog! Good sit!', etc. Remember to always praise enthusiastically, because dogs relish verbal praise from their owners and feel so proud of themselves whenever they accomplish a behaviour.

go to you and pay attention; if he does, he will get to interact with you plus receive treats and praise.

THE BASIC COMMANDS
TEACHING SIT
Now that you have the dog's attention, attach his lead and hold it in your left hand and a food treat in your right. Place your food hand at the dog's nose and let him lick the treat but not take it from you. Say 'Sit' and slowly raise

You will not use food forever in getting the dog to obey your commands. Food is only used to teach new behaviours, and once the dog knows what you want when you give a specific command, you will wean him off of the food treats but still maintain the verbal praise. After all, you will always have your voice with you, and there will be many times when you have no food rewards but expect the dog to obey.

TEACHING DOWN
Teaching the down exercise is easy when you understand how the dog perceives the down position, and it is very difficult when you do not. Dogs perceive the down position as a submissive one, therefore teaching the down exercise using a forceful method can sometimes make the dog develop such a fear of the down

The Success Method

Success that comes by luck is usually short lived. Success that comes by well-thought-out proven methods is often more easily achieved and permanent. This is the Success Method. It is designed to give you, the puppy owner, a simple yet proven way to help your puppy develop clean living habits and a feeling of security in his new environment.

Teaching your Sheltie to sit and stay is simple. Note that the trainer has her foot on the lead to keep control of the situation.

hand there so you can guide the dog to lie down close to your left leg rather than to swing away from your side when he drops.

Now place the food hand at the dog's nose, say 'Down' very softly (almost a whisper), and slowly lower the food hand to the dog's front feet. When the food

Teaching the down exercise is more difficult than the sit exercise because down is a submissive position for a dog.

that he either runs away when you say 'Down' or he attempts to snap at the person who tries to force him down.

Have the dog sit close along-side your left leg, facing in the same direction as you are. Hold the lead in your left hand and a food treat in your right. Now place your left hand lightly on the top of the dog's shoulders where they meet above the spinal cord. Do not push down on the dog's shoulders; simply rest your left

Obedience School

A basic obedience beginner's class usually lasts for six to eight weeks. Dog and owner attend an hour-long lesson once a week and practice for a few minutes, several times a day, each day at home. If done properly, the whole procedure will result in a well-mannered dog and an owner who delights in living with a pet that is eager to please and enjoys doing things with his owner.

Begin teaching the stay command from a close distance. As you and your Sheltie progress, you can increase the distance between the two of you.

hand reaches the floor, begin moving it forward along the floor in front of the dog. Keep talking softly to the dog, saying things like, 'Do you want this treat? You can do this, good dog.' Your reassuring tone of voice will help calm the dog as he tries to follow the food hand in order to get the treat.

When the dog's elbows touch the floor, release the food and praise softly. Try to get the dog to maintain that down position for several seconds before you let him sit up again. The goal here is to get the dog to settle down and not feel threatened in the down position.

TEACHING STAY

It is easy to teach the dog to stay in either a sit or a down position. Again, we use food and praise during the teaching process as we help the dog to understand exactly what it is that we are expecting him to do.

Did You Know?

A dog in jeopardy never lies down. He stays alert on his feet because instinct tells him that he may have to run away or fight for his survival. Therefore, if a dog feels threatened or anxious, he will not lie down. Consequently, it is important to have the dog calm and relaxed as he learns the down exercise.

To teach the sit/stay, start with the dog sitting on your left side as before and hold the lead in your left hand. Have a food treat in your right hand and place your food hand at the dog's nose. Say 'Stay' and step out on your right foot to stand directly in front of the dog, toe to toe, as he licks and nibbles the treat. Be sure to keep his head facing upward to maintain the sit position. Count to five and then swing around to stand next to the dog again with him on your left. As soon as you get back to the origi-

nal position, release the food and praise lavishly.

To teach the down/stay, do the down as previously described. As soon as the dog lies down, say 'Stay' and step out on your right foot just as you did in the sit/stay. Count to five and then return to stand beside the dog with him on your left side. Release the treat and praise as always.

Within a week or ten days, you can begin to add a bit of distance between you and your dog when you leave him. When you do, use your left hand open with the palm facing the dog as a stay signal, much the same as the hand signal a police officer uses to stop traffic at an intersection. Hold the food treat in your right hand as before, but this time the food is not touching the dog's nose. He will watch the food hand and quickly learn that he is going to get that treat as soon as you return to his side.

When you can stand 1 metre

away from your dog for 30 seconds, you can then begin building time and distance in both stays. Eventually, the dog can be expected to remain in the stay position for prolonged periods of time until you return to him or call him to you. Always praise lavishly when he stays.

Teaching Come

If you make teaching 'come' a fun experience, you should never have a 'student' that does not love the game or that fails to come when called. The secret, it seems, is never to teach the word 'come.'

At times when an owner most wants his dog to come when called, the owner is likely upset or anxious and he allows these feelings to come through in the tone of his voice when he calls his dog. Hearing that desperation in his owner's voice, the dog fears the results of going to him and

When teaching the stay command, or any other command, make sure that you and your Shetland Sheepdog are relaxed and not distracted. If the dog feels pressure or your insecurity, he will not perform well and not enjoy the sessions.

Did You Know?

If you start with a normal, healthy dog and give him time, patience and some carefully executed lessons, you will reap the rewards of that training for the life of the dog. And what a life it will be! The two of you will find immeasurable pleasure in the companionship you have built together with love, respect and understanding. Good luck and enjoy!

therefore either disobeys outright or runs in the opposite direction. The secret, therefore, is to teach the dog a game and, when you want him to come to you, simply play the game. It is practically a no-fail solution!

To begin, have several mem-

Since Shelties love to please their masters, the 'come' command does not pose as great a challenge as it does with other breeds. Using a ball or a treat makes the exercise even simpler.

> ### Training Tip
>
> Never train your dog, puppy or adult, when you are mad or in a sour mood. Dogs are very sensitive to human feelings, especially anger, and if your dog senses that you are angry or upset, he will connect your anger with his training and learn to resent or fear his training sessions.

bers of your family take a few food treats and each go into a different room in the house. Take turns calling the dog, and each person should celebrate the dog's finding him with a treat and lots of happy praise. When a person calls the dog, he is actually inviting the dog to find him and get a treat as a reward for 'winning.'

A few turns of the 'Where are you?' game and the dog will figure out that everyone is playing the game and that each person has a big celebration awaiting his success at locating them. Once he learns to love the game, simply calling out 'Where are you?' will bring him running from wherever he is when he hears that all-important question.

The come command is recognised as one of the most important things to teach a dog, but there are trainers who work with thousands of dogs and never teach the actual word 'Come.' Yet these dogs will race to respond to a per-

> ### Training Tip
>
> Never call your dog to come to you for a correction or scold him when he reaches you. That is the quickest way to turn a 'Come' command into 'Go away fast!' Dogs think only in the present tense, and your dog will connect the scolding with coming to you, not with the misbehaviour of a few moments earlier.

son who uses the dog's name followed by 'Where are you?' For example, a woman has a 12-year-old companion dog who went blind, but who never fails to locate her owner when asked, 'Where are you?'

Children particularly love to play this game with their dogs. Children can hide in smaller places like a shower or bathtub, behind a bed or under a table. The dog needs to work a little bit harder to find these hiding places, but when he does he loves to celebrate with a treat and a tussle with a favourite youngster.

TEACHING HEEL

Heeling means that the dog walks beside the owner without pulling. Most Shelties have no problem whatsoever in learning to walk on a lead precisely at the owner's side. This is true for a herding dog that learns that the owner is the master and that he belongs by his

Herding dogs excel at learning to walk alongside their owners, although some dogs tend to lead the way. Your Sheltie must learn to walk by your side, regardless of your pace, without exerting any pressure on his lead.

Training Tip

When calling the dog, do not say 'Come.' Say things like, 'Rover, where are you? See if you can find me! I have a cookie for you!' Keep up a constant line of chatter with coaxing sounds and frequent questions such as, 'Where are you?' The dog will learn to follow the sound of your voice to locate you and receive his reward.

A Sheltie, properly trained to heel, will stop when you stop walking, and then sit at your side until you resume walking again.

Training Tip

If you are walking your dog and he suddenly stops and looks straight into your eyes, ignore him. Pull the leash and lead him into the direction you want to walk.

Training Tip

If you begin teaching the heel by taking long walks and letting the dog pull you along, he misinterprets this action as an acceptable form of taking a walk. When you pull back on the lead to counteract his pulling, he reads that tug as a signal to pull even harder!

master's side. Whilst many dog owners struggle with this exercise, Sheltie owners should revel in their dog's natural instincts and intelligence.

Begin with holding the lead in your left hand as the dog sits beside your left leg. Move the loop end of the lead to your right hand but keep your left hand short on the lead so it keeps the dog in close next to you.

Say 'Heel' and step forward on your left foot. Keep the dog close to you and take three steps. Stop and have the dog sit next to you in what we now call the 'heel position.' Praise verbally, but do not touch the dog. Hesitate a moment and begin again with 'Heel,' taking three steps and stopping, at which point the dog is told to sit again.

Your goal here is to have the dog walk those three steps without pulling on the lead. When he will walk calmly beside you for three steps without pulling, increase the number of steps you take to five. When he will walk politely beside you whilst you take five steps, you can increase the length of your walk to ten steps. Keep increasing the length of your stroll until the dog will walk quietly beside you without pulling as long as you want him to heel. When you stop heeling, indicate to the dog that the exercise is over by verbally praising as you pet him and say 'OK, good dog.' The 'OK' is used as a release word meaning that the exercise is finished and the dog is free to relax.

If you are dealing with a dog who insists on pulling you around, simply 'put on your brakes' and stand your ground until the dog realises that the two of you are not going anywhere until he is beside you and moving at your pace, not his. It may take some time just standing there to convince the dog that you are the leader and you will be the one to decide on the direction and speed of your travel.

Each time the dog looks up at you or slows down to give a slack lead between the two of you, quietly praise him and say, 'Good heel. Good dog.' Eventually, the dog will begin to respond and within a few days he will be walking politely beside you without pulling on the lead. At first, the training sessions should be kept short and very positive; soon the dog will be able to walk nicely with you for increasingly longer distances. Remember also to give the dog free time and the opportunity to run and play when you are done with heel practice.

> ### Training Tip
>
> Teach your dog to HEEL in an enclosed area. Once you think the dog will obey reliably and you want to attempt advanced obedience exercises such as off-lead heeling, test him in a fenced-in area so he cannot run away.

WEANING OFF FOOD IN TRAINING

Food is used in training new behaviours. Once the dog understands what behaviour goes with a specific command, it is time to start weaning him off the food treats. At first, give a treat after each exercise. Then, start to give a treat only after every other exercise. Mix up the times when you offer a food reward and the times when you only offer praise so that the dog will never know when he is going to receive both food and praise and when he is going to receive only praise. This is called a variable ratio reward system and it proves successful because there is always the chance that the owner will produce a treat, so the dog never stops trying for that reward. No matter what, ALWAYS give verbal praise.

OBEDIENCE CLASSES

It is a good idea to enrol in an obedience class if one is available in your area. If yours is a show dog, ringcraft classes would be more appropriate. Many areas have dog clubs that offer basic obedience training as well as preparatory classes for obedience competition. There are also local dog trainers who offer similar classes.

At obedience trials, dogs can earn titles at various levels of competition. The beginning levels of competition include basic behaviours such as sit, down, heel, etc. The more advanced levels of competition include jumping, retrieving, scent discrimination and signal work. The advanced levels require a dog and owner to put a lot of time and effort into their training and the titles that can be earned at these levels of competition are very prestigious.

OTHER ACTIVITIES FOR LIFE
Whether a dog is trained in the structured environment of a class or alone with his owner at home, there are many activities that can bring fun and rewards to both owner and dog once they have mastered basic control.

Teaching the dog to help out around the home, in the garden or on the farm provides great satisfaction to both dog and owner. In addition, the dog's help makes life a little easier for his owner and raises his stature as a valued companion to his family. It helps give the dog a purpose by occupying his mind and providing an outlet for his energy.

Backpacking is an exciting and healthy activity that the dog can be taught without assistance from more than his owner. The exercise of walking and climbing is good for man and dog alike, and the bond that they develop together is priceless.

If you are interested in participating in organised competition with your Shetland Sheepdog, there are activities other than obedience in which you and your dog can become involved. Agility is a popular and fun sport where dogs run through an obstacle course that includes various jumps, tunnels and other exercises to test the dog's speed and coordination. The owners run through the course beside their dogs to give commands and to guide them through the course. Although competitive, the focus is on fun—it's fun to do, fun to watch, and great exercise.

Obedience School

Taking your dog to an obedience school may be the best investment in time and money you can ever make. You will enjoy the benefits for the lifetime of your dog and you will have the opportunity to meet people with your similar expectations for companion dogs.

First Aid at a Glance

Burns
Place the affected area under cool water; use ice if only a small area is burnt.

Bee/Insect bites
Apply ice to relieve swelling; antihistamine dosed properly.

Animal bites
Clean any bleeding area; apply pressure until bleeding subsides; go to the vet.

Spider bites
Use cold compress and a pressurised pack to inhibit venom's spreading.

Antifreeze poisoning
Immediately induce vomiting by using hydrogen peroxide.

Fish hooks
Removal best handled by vet; hook must be cut in order to remove.

Snake bites
Pack ice around bite; contact vet quickly; identify snake for proper antivenin.

Car accident
Move dog from roadway with blanket; seek veterinary aid.

Shock
Calm the dog, keep him warm; seek immediate veterinary help.

Nosebleed
Apply cold compress to the nose; apply pressure to any visible abrasion.

Bleeding
Apply pressure above the area; treat wound by applying a cotton pack.

Heat stroke
Submerge dog in cold bath; cool down with fresh air and water; go to the vet.

Frostbite/Hypothermia
Warm the dog with a warm bath, electric blankets or hot water bottles.

Abrasions
Clean the wound and wash out thoroughly with fresh water; apply antiseptic.

Remember: an injured dog may attempt to bite a helping hand from fear and confusion. Always muzzle the dog before trying to offer assistance.

Dogs suffer many of the same physical illnesses as people. They might even share many of the same psychological problems. Since people usually know more about human diseases than canine maladies, many of the terms used in this chapter will be familiar but not necessarily those used by veterinary surgeons. We will use the term *x-ray*, instead of the more acceptable term *radiograph*. We will also use the familiar term *symptoms* even though dogs don't have symptoms, which are verbal descriptions of the patient's feelings: dogs have *clinical signs*. Since dogs can't speak, we have to look for clinical signs...but we still use the term symptoms in this book.

As a general rule, medicine is practised. That term is not arbitrary. Medicine is a constantly changing art as we learn more and more about genetics, electronic aids (like CAT scans) and daily laboratory advances. There are many dog maladies, like canine hip dysplasia, which are not universally treated in the same manner. Some veterinary surgeons opt for surgery more often than others do.

SELECTING A VETERINARY SURGEON
Your selection of a veterinary surgeon should not be based upon personality (as most are) but upon their convenience to your home. You want a vet who is close because you might have emergencies or need to make multiple visits for treatments. You want a vet who has services that you might require such as a boarding kennel and grooming facilities, as well as sophisticated pet supplies and a good reputation for ability and responsiveness. There is nothing more frustrating than having to wait a day or more to get a response from your veterinary surgeon.

Before you buy your Shetland Sheepdog, meet and interview the veterinary surgeons in your area. Take everything into consideration—discuss his background, specialities, fees, emergency policy, etc.

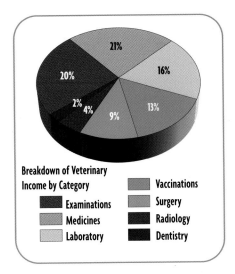

Breakdown of Veterinary Income by Category

- Examinations
- Medicines
- Laboratory
- Vaccinations
- Surgery
- Radiology
- Dentistry

A typical American vet's income categorised according to services performed. This survey dealt with small-animal (pet) practices.

dent to get another medical opinion, although in Britain you are obliged to advise the vets concerned about this. You might also want to compare costs amongst several veterinary surgeons. Sophisticated health care and veterinary services can be very costly. Don't be bashful about discussing these costs with your veterinary surgeon or his (her) staff. It is not infrequent that important decisions are based upon financial considerations.

PREVENTATIVE MEDICINE

It is much easier, less costly and more effective to practise preventative medicine than to fight bouts of illness and disease. Properly bred puppies come from parents that were selected based upon their genetic disease profile. Their mothers should have been vaccinated, free of all internal and external parasites, and properly nourished. For these reasons, a visit to the veterinary surgeon who cared for the dam (mother) is recommended. The dam can pass on disease resistance to her puppies, which can last for eight to ten weeks. She can also pass on parasites and many infections. That's why you should visit the veterinary surgeon who cared for the dam.

WEANING TO FIVE MONTHS OLD

Puppies should be weaned by the time they are about two months

All veterinary surgeons are licensed and their diplomas and/or certificates should be displayed in their waiting rooms. There are, however, many veterinary specialities that usually require further studies and internships. There are specialists in heart problems (veterinary cardiologists), skin problems (veterinary dermatologists), teeth and gum problems (veterinary dentists), eye problems (veterinary ophthalmologists), X-rays (veterinary radiologists), and surgeons who have specialities in bones, muscles or other organs. Most veterinary surgeons do routine surgery such as neutering, stitching up wounds and docking tails for those breeds in which such is required for show purposes. When the problem affecting your dog is serious, it is not unusual or impu-

old. A puppy that remains for at least eight weeks with its mother and littermates usually adapts better to other dogs and people later in its life.

Some new owners have their puppy examined by a veterinary surgeon immediately, which is a good idea. Vaccination programmes usually begin when the puppy is very young.

The puppy will have its teeth examined and have its skeletal conformation and general health checked prior to certification by the veterinary surgeon. Puppies in certain breeds have problems with their kneecaps, eye cataracts and other eye problems, heart murmurs and undescended testicles. They may also have personality problems and your veterinary surgeon might have training in temperament evaluation.

VACCINATION SCHEDULING
Most vaccinations are given by injection and should only be done by a vet-

Did You Know?

Cases of hyperactive adrenal glands (Cushing's disease) have been traced to the drinking of highly chlorinated water. Aerate or age your dog's drinking water before offering it.

erinary surgeon. Both he and you should keep a record of the date of the injection, the identification of the vaccine and the amount given. Some vets give a first vaccination at eight weeks, but most dog breeders prefer the course not to commence until about ten weeks because of negating any antibodies passed on by the dam. The vaccination scheduling is usually based on a 15-day cycle. You must take your vet's advice as to when to vaccinate as this may differ according to the vaccine used. Most vaccinations immunise your puppy against viruses.

The usual vaccines contain immunising doses of several different viruses such as distemper, parvovirus, parainfluenza and hepatitis. There are other vaccines available when the puppy is at risk. You should rely upon professional advice. This is especially true for the booster-shot programme. Most vaccination programmes require a booster when the puppy is a year old and once a year there-

Did You Know?

Your veterinary surgeon will probably recommend that your puppy be vaccinated before you take him outside. There are airborne diseases, parasite eggs in the grass and unexpected visits from other dogs that might be dangerous to your puppy's health.

Normal Shetland Sheepdog Skeleton

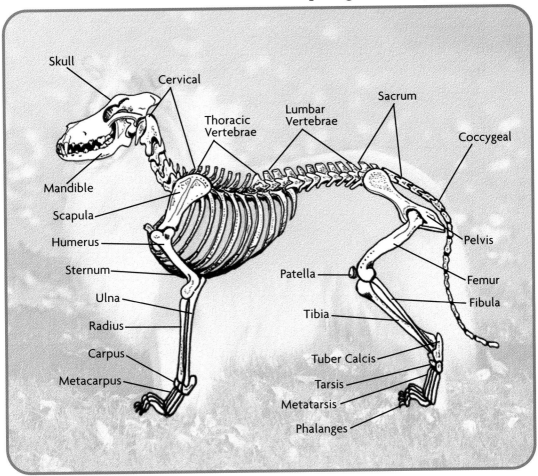

Skull

Cervical

Sacrum

Thoracic
Vertebrae

Lumbar
Vertebrae

Coccygeal

Mandible

Scapula

Humerus

Sternum

Patella

Ulna

Radius

Carpus

Metacarpus

Pelvis

Femur

Fibula

Tibia

Tuber Calcis

Tarsis

Metatarsis

Phalanges

after. In some cases, circumstances may require more frequent immunisations. Kennel cough, more formally known as tracheobronchitis, is treated with a vaccine that is sprayed into the dog's nostrils. Kennel cough is usually included in routine vaccination, but this is often not so effective as for other major diseases.

Did You Know?

Not every dog's ears are the same. Ears that are open to the air are healthier than ears with poor air circulation. Sometimes a dog can have two differently shaped ears. You should not probe inside your dog's ears. Only clean that which is accessible with a soft cotton wipe.

HEALTH AND VACCINATION SCHEDULE

AGE IN WEEKS:	3RD	6TH	8TH	10TH	12TH	14TH	16TH	20-24TH
Worm Control	✔	✔	✔	✔	✔	✔	✔	✔
Neutering								✔
Heartworm*		✔						✔
Parvovirus		✔		✔		✔		✔
Distemper			✔		✔		✔	
Hepatitis			✔		✔		✔	
Leptospirosis		✔		✔		✔		
Parainfluenza		✔		✔		✔		
Dental Examination			✔					✔
Complete Physical			✔					✔
Temperament Testing			✔					
Coronavirus					✔			
Kennel Cough		✔						
Hip Dysplasia							✔	
Rabies*								✔

Vaccinations are not instantly effective. It takes about two weeks for the dog's immunisation system to develop antibodies. Most vaccinations require annual booster shots. Your veterinary surgeon should guide you in this regard.
*Not applicable in the United Kingdom

FIVE MONTHS TO ONE YEAR OF AGE
Unless you intend to breed or show your dog, neutering the puppy at six months of age is recommended. Discuss this with your veterinary surgeon. Most professionals advise neutering the puppy. Neutering has proven to be extremely beneficial to both male and female puppies. Besides eliminating the possibility of pregnancy, it inhibits (but does not prevent) breast cancer in bitches and prostate cancer in male dogs. Under no circumstances should a bitch be spayed prior to her first season.

DOGS OLDER THAN ONE YEAR
Continue to visit the veterinary surgeon at least once a year. There

Did You Know?

Vaccines do not work all the time. Sometimes dogs are allergic to them and many times the antibodies, which are supposed to be stimulated by the vaccine, just are not produced. You should keep your dog in the veterinary clinic for an hour after it is vaccinated to be sure there are no allergic reactions.

is no such disease as old age, but bodily functions do change with age. The eyes and ears are no longer as efficient. Liver, kidney and intestinal functions often decline. Proper dietary changes, recommended by your veterinary surgeon, can make life more pleasant for the ageing Shetland Sheepdog and you.

SKIN PROBLEMS IN SHETLAND SHEEPDOGS

Veterinary surgeons are consulted by dog owners for skin problems more than any other group of diseases or maladies. Dogs' skin is almost as sensitive as human skin and both suffer almost the same ailments (though the occurrence of acne in dogs is rare!). For this reason, veterinary dermatology has developed into a speciality practised by many veterinary surgeons.

Since many skin problems have visual symptoms that are almost identical, it requires the skill of an experienced veterinary dermatologist to identify and cure many of the more severe skin disorders. Pet shops sell many treatments for skin problems but most of the treatments are directed at symptoms and not the underlying problem(s). If your dog is suffering from a skin disorder, you should seek professional assis-

Disease	What is it?	What causes it?	Symptoms
Leptospirosis	Severe disease that affects the internal organs; can be spread to people.	A bacterium, which is often carried by rodents, that enters through mucous membranes and spreads quickly throughout the body.	Range from fever, vomiting and loss of appetite in less severe cases to shock, irreversible kidney damage and possibly death in most severe cases.
Rabies	Potentially deadly virus that infects warm-blooded mammals. Not seen in United Kingdom.	Bite from a carrier of the virus, mainly wild animals.	1st stage: dog exhibits change in behaviour, fear. 2nd stage: dog's behaviour becomes more aggressive. 3rd stage: loss of coordination, trouble with bodily functions.
Parvovirus	Highly contagious virus, potentially deadly.	Ingestion of the virus, which is usually spread through the faeces of infected dogs.	Most common: severe diarrhoea. Also vomiting, fatigue, lack of appetite.
Kennel cough	Contagious respiratory infection.	Combination of types of bacteria and virus. Most common: *Bordetella bronchiseptica* bacteria and parainfluenza virus.	Chronic cough.
Distemper	Disease primarily affecting respiratory and nervous system.	Virus that is related to the human measles virus.	Mild symptoms such as fever, lack of appetite and mucous secretion progress to evidence of brain damage, 'hard pad.'
Hepatitis	Virus primarily affecting the liver.	Canine adenovirus type I (CAV-1). Enters system when dog breathes in particles.	Lesser symptoms include listlessness, diarrhoea, vomiting. More severe symptoms include 'blue-eye' (clumps of virus in eye).
Coronavirus	Virus resulting in digestive problems.	Virus is spread through infected dog's faeces.	Stomach upset evidenced by lack of appetite, vomiting, diarrhoea.

tance as quickly as possible. As with all diseases, the earlier a problem is identified and treated, the more successful is the cure.

INHERITED SKIN PROBLEMS

Many skin disorders are inherited and some are fatal. For example, acrodermatitis is an inherited disease that is transmitted by both parents. The parents, who appear (phenotypically) normal, have a recessive gene for acrodermatitis, meaning that they carry, but are not affected by the disease.

Acrodermatitis is just one example of how difficult it is to prevent congenital dog diseases. The cost and skills required to ascertain whether two dogs should be mated are too high even though puppies with acrodermatitis rarely reach two years of age.

Other inherited skin problems are usually not as fatal as acrodermatitis. All inherited diseases must be diagnosed and treated by a veterinary specialist. There are active programmes being undertaken by many veterinary pharmaceutical manufacturers to solve most, if not all, of the common skin problems of dogs.

PARASITE BITES

Many of us are allergic to insect bites. The bites itch, erupt and may even become infected. Dogs have the same reaction to fleas, ticks and/or mites. When an insect lands on you, you have the chance to whisk it

Did You Know?

There is a 25% chance of a puppy getting this fatal gene combination from two parents with recessive genes for acrodermatitis:

AA= NORMAL, HEALTHY
aa= FATAL
Aa= RECESSIVE, NORMAL APPEARING

If the female parent has an Aa gene and the male parent has an Aa gene, the chances are one in four that the puppy will have the fatal genetic combination aa.

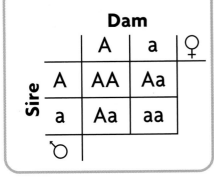

AUTO-IMMUNE SKIN CONDITIONS

Auto-immune skin conditions are commonly referred to as being allergic to yourself, whilst allergies are usually inflammatory reactions to an outside stimulus. Auto-immune diseases cause serious damage to the tissues that are involved.

The best known auto-immune disease is lupus, which affects people as well as dogs. The symptoms are variable and may affect the kidneys, bones, blood chemistry and skin. It can be fatal to both dogs and humans, though it is not thought to be transmissible. It is usually successfully treated with cortisone, prednisone or similar corticosteroid, but extensive use of these drugs can have harmful side effects.

HOT SPOTS/LICK GRANULOMA

Many dogs have a very poorly understood condition known as a lick granuloma or a hot spot. The manifestation of the problem is the dog's tireless attack at a specific area of the body, almost always the legs or paws. They lick so intensively that

away with your hand. Unfortunately, when our dog is bitten by a flea, tick or mite, it can only scratch it away or bite it. By the time the dog has been bitten, the parasite has done some of its damage. It may also have laid eggs to cause further problems in the near future. The itching from parasite bites is probably due to the saliva injected into the site when the parasite sucks the dog's blood.

Did You Know?

Feeding your dog properly is very important. An incorrect diet could affect the dog's health, behaviour and nervous system, possibly making a normal dog into an aggressive one.

they remove the hair and skin leaving an ugly, large wound. Owners who notice their dogs' biting and chewing at their extremities should have the vet determine the cause. If lick granuloma is the cause, although there is no absolute cure, corticosteroids are the most common treatment. Hot spots are common on coated breeds like the Shetland Sheepdog especially during the summer months. Similar treatment is available through your vet.

AIRBORNE ALLERGIES

An interesting allergy is pollen allergy. Humans have hay fever, rose fever and other fevers with which they suffer during the pollinating season. Many dogs suffer the same allergies. When the pollen count is high, your dog might suffer but don't expect them to sneeze and have runny noses like humans. Dogs react to pollen allergies the same way they react to fleas—they scratch and bite themselves.

Dogs, like humans, can be

Especially in the warm months, coated breeds like Shelties can suffer from fleas, hot spots and other haircoat-related problems. Owners must check over their dogs carefully and be prepared to prevent and treat these problems.

tested for allergens. Discuss the testing with your veterinary dermatologist.

FOOD PROBLEMS
FOOD ALLERGIES
Dogs are allergic to many foods that are best-sellers and highly recommended by breeders and veterinary surgeons. Changing the brand of food that you buy may not eliminate the problem if the element to which the dog is allergic is contained in the new brand.

Recognising a food allergy is difficult. Humans vomit or have rashes when they eat a food to which they are allergic. Dogs neither vomit nor (usually) develop a rash. They react in the same manner as they do to an airborne or flea allergy: they itch, scratch and bite, thus making the diagnosis extremely difficult. Whilst pollen allergies and parasite bites are usually seasonal, food allergies are year-round problems.

FOOD INTOLERANCE
Food intolerance is the inability of the dog to completely digest certain foods. Puppies that may have done very well on their mother's milk may not do well on cow's milk. The result of this food intolerance may be loose bowels, passing gas and stomach pains. These are the only obvious symptoms of food intolerance and that makes diagnosis difficult.

TREATING FOOD PROBLEMS
It is possible to handle food allergies and food intolerance yourself. Put your dog on a diet that it has never had. Obviously if it has never eaten this new food it can't have been allergic or intolerant of it. Start with a single ingredient that is not in the dog's diet at the present time. Ingredients like chopped beef or fish are common in dog's diets, so try something more exotic like rabbit, pheasant or even just vegetables. Keep the dog on this diet (with no additives) for a month. If the symptoms of food allergy or intolerance disappear, chances are your dog has a food allergy.

Don't think that the single ingredient cured the problem. You still must find a suitable diet and ascertain which ingredient in the old diet was objectionable. This is most easily done by adding ingredients to the new diet one at a time. Let the dog stay on the modified diet for a month before you add another ingredient. An alternative method is to carefully study the ingredients in the diet to which your dog is allergic or intolerant. Identify the main ingredient in this diet and eliminate the main ingredient by buying a different food that does not have that ingredient. Keep experimenting until the symptoms disappear after one month on the new diet.

A scanning electron micrograph (S. E. M.) of a dog flea, *Ctenocephalides canis.*

S. E. M. BY DR DENNIS KUNKEL, UNIVERSITY OF HAWAII

EXTERNAL PARASITES

Opposite page: A scanning electron micrograph of a dog or cat flea, *Ctenocephalides*, magnified more than 100x. This has been colourised for effect.

Of all the problems to which dogs are prone, none is more well known and frustrating than fleas. Flea infestation, is relatively simple to cure but difficult to prevent. Parasites that are

harboured inside the body are a bit more difficult to eradicate but they are easier to control.

FLEAS

To control a flea infestation you have to understand the flea's life cycle. Fleas are often thought of as a summertime problem but centrally heated homes have changed the patterns and fleas can be found at any time of the year. The most effective method of flea control is a two-stage approach: one stage to kill the adult fleas, and the other to control the development of pre-adult fleas. Unfortunately, no single active ingredient is effective against all stages of the life cycle.

LIFE CYCLE STAGES

During its life, a flea will pass through four life stages: egg, larva, pupa and adult. The adult stage is the most visible and irritating stage of the flea life cycle

Did You Know?

Fleas have been around for millions of years and have adapted to changing host animals.

Magnified head of a dog flea, *Ctenocephalides canis.*

They are able to go through a complete life cycle in less than one month or they can extend their lives to almost two years by remaining as pupae or cocoons. They do not need blood or any other food for up to 20 months.

They have been measured as being able to jump 300,000 times and can jump 150 times their length in any direction including straight up. Those are just a few of the reasons they are so successful in infesting a dog!

S. E. M. BY DR DENNIS KUNKEL, UNIVERSITY OF HAWAII

The Life Cycle of the Flea

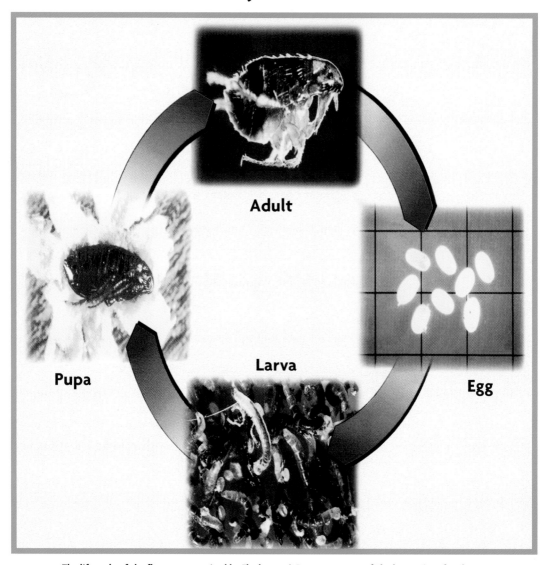

Adult

Pupa

Larva

Egg

The life cycle of the flea was posterised by Fleabusters®. Poster courtesy of Fleabusters®, R$_x$ for Fleas.

and this is why the majority of flea-control products concentrate on this stage. The fact is that adult fleas account for only 1% of the total flea population, and the other 99% exist in pre-adult stages, i.e., eggs, larvae and pupae. These pre-adult stages are barely visible to the naked eye.

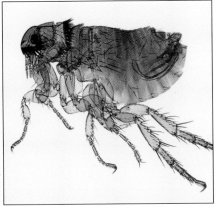

PHOTO BY JEAN CLAUDE REVY/PHOTOTAKE.

THE LIFE CYCLE OF THE FLEA

Eggs are laid on the dog, usually in quantities of about 20 or 30 a day. The female adult flea must have a blood meal before each egg-laying session. The eggs will quickly dry out and fall from the dog, especially as the dog moves around or scratches. Many eggs will fall off in the dog's favourite area or an area in which he spends a lot of time, such as his bed or any items of furniture the dog may use.

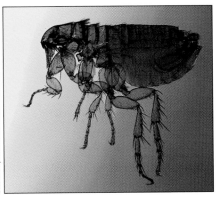

PHOTO BY JEAN CLAUDE REVY/PHOTOTAKE.

On Guard: Catching Fleas Off Guard

Consider the following ways to arm yourself against fleas:
• Add a small amount of pennyroyal or eucalyptus oil to your dog's bath. These natural remedies repel fleas.
• Supplement your dog's food with fresh garlic (minced or grated) and a hearty amount of brewer's yeast, both of which ward off fleas.
• Use a flea comb on your dog daily. Submerge fleas in a cup of bleach to kill them quickly.
• Confine the dog to only a few rooms to limit the spread of fleas in the home.
• Vacuum daily...and get all of the crevices! Dispose of the bag every few days until the problem is under control.
• Wash your dog's bedding daily. Cover cushions where your dog sleeps with towels, and wash the towels often.

A male dog flea, *Ctenocephalides canis*.

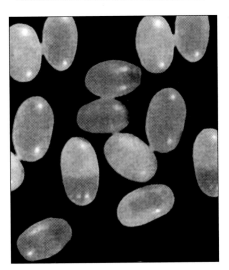

The eggs of the dog flea.

Male cat fleas, *Ctenocephalides felis*, are very commonly found on dogs.

Once the eggs fall from the dog onto the carpet or furniture, they will hatch into larvae. This takes from one to ten days. Larvae are not particularly mobile, and will usually travel only a few inches from where they hatch. However, they do have a tendency to move downwards away from light—under furniture and behind doors are common places to find high quantities of flea larvae.

The flea larvae feed on dead organic matter, including adult flea faeces, until they are ready to change into adult fleas. Fleas will usually remain as larvae for around seven days. After this period, the larvae will pupate into protective pupae. While inside the pupae, the larvae will undergo metamorphosis and change into adult fleas. This can take as little time as a few days, but the adult fleas can remain inside the pupae

waiting to hatch for up to two years. The pupae are signalled to hatch by certain stimuli, such as physical pressure—the pupae's being stepped on, heat from an animal lying on the pupae or increased carbon dioxide levels and vibrations—indicating that a suitable host is available.

Once hatched, the adult flea can wait a few weeks to find a host. When the adult flea finds a host, it will not leave voluntarily. It only becomes dislodged by grooming or the host animal's scratching. The adult flea will remain on the host for the duration of its life unless forcibly removed.

TREATING THE ENVIRONMENT AND THE DOG

Treating fleas should be a two-pronged attack. First, the environment needs to be treated; this includes carpets and furniture, especially the dog's bedding and areas underneath fur-

118

Did You Know?

Never mix flea control products without first consulting your veterinary surgeon. Some products can become toxic when combined with others and can cause serious or fatal consequences.

niture. The environment should be treated with a household spray containing an Insect Growth Regulator (IGR) and an insecticide to kill the adult flea. Most IGRs are effective against eggs and larvae. They actually stop the eggs and larvae from developing into adult fleas. There are currently no treatments available to attack the pupa stage of the life cycle, so the adult insecticide is used to kill the newly hatched adult fleas before they find a host. Most IGRs are active for many months, whilst adult insecticides are only active for a few days.

When treating with a household spray, it is a good idea to vacuum before applying the product. This stimulates as many pupae as possible to hatch into adult fleas. The vacuum cleaner should also be treated with a flea treatment to prevent the eggs and larvae that have been hoovered into the vacuum bag from hatching.

The second stage of treatment is to apply an adult insec-

ticide to the dog. Traditionally, this would be in the form of a collar or a spray, but more recent innovations include injection insecticides that poison the fleas when they ingest the dog's blood. Alternatively, there are drops that, when placed on the back of the animal's neck, spread throughout the fur and skin to kill adult fleas.

Did You Know?

Two types of products should be used when treating fleas—a product to treat the pet and a product to treat the home. Adult fleas represent less than 1% of the flea population. The pre-adult fleas (eggs, larvae and pupae) represent more than 99% of the flea population and are found in the environment; it is in the case of pre-adult fleas that products containing an Insect Growth Regulator (IGR) should be used in the home.

IGRs are a new class of compounds used to prevent the development of insects. They do not kill the insect outright, but instead use the insect's biology against it to stop it from completing its growth. Products that contain methoprene are the world's first and leading IGRs. Used to control fleas and other insects, this type of IGR will stop flea larvae from developing and protect the house for up to seven months.

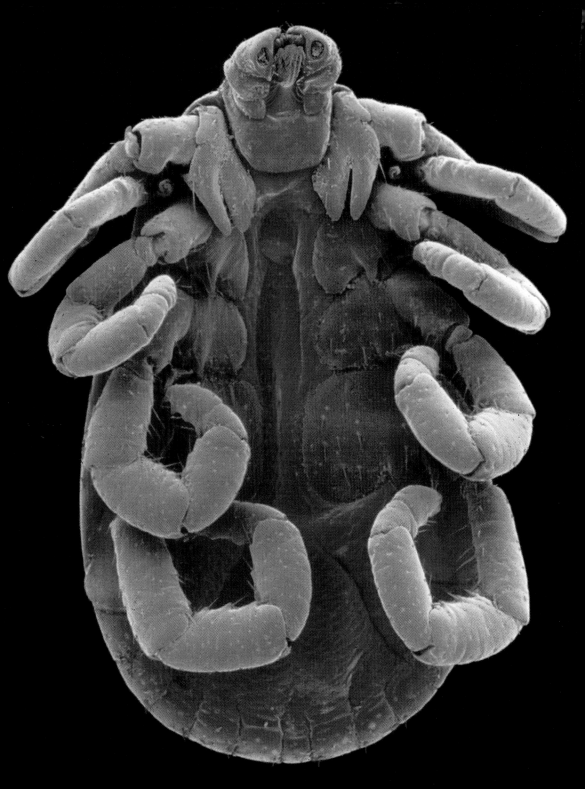

TICKS AND MITES

Though not as common as fleas, ticks and mites are found all over the tropical and temperate world. They don't bite, like fleas; they harpoon. They dig their sharp proboscis (nose) into the dog's skin and drink the blood. Their only food and drink is dog's blood. Dogs can get Lyme disease, Rocky Mountain spotted fever (normally found in the USA only), paralysis and many other diseases from ticks and mites. They may live where fleas are found and they like to hide in cracks or seams in walls wherever dogs live. They are controlled the same way fleas are controlled.

The dog tick, *Dermacentor variabilis*, may well be the most common dog tick in many geographical areas, especially those areas where the climate is hot and humid.

Most dog ticks have life

PHOTO BY JEAN CLAUDE REVY/PHOTOTAKE

expectancies of a week to six months, depending upon climatic conditions. They can neither jump nor fly, but they can crawl slowly and can range up to 5 metres (16 feet) to reach a sleeping or unsuspecting dog.

MANGE

Mites cause a skin irritation called mange. Some are contagious, like *Cheyletiella*, ear mites, scabies and chiggers. The non-contagious mites are *Demodex*. Mites that cause ear-mite infestation are usually controlled with ivermectin, which is often toxic to Collies and probably should be avoided in all herding breeds.

It is essential that your dog be treated for mange as quickly as possible because some forms of mange are transmissible to people.

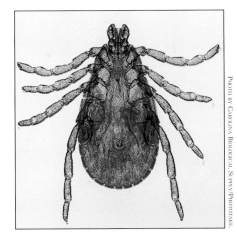

PHOTO BY CAROLINA BIOLOGICAL SUPPLY/PHOTOTAKE.

S. E. M. BY DR DENNIS KUNKEL, UNIVERSITY OF HAWAII.

An uncommon dog tick of the genus *Ixode*. Magnified 10x.

Opposite page: The dog tick, *Dermacentor variabilis*, is probably the most common tick found on dogs. Look at the strength in its eight legs! No wonder it's hard to detach them.

A brown dog tick, *Rhipicephalus sanguineus*, is an uncommon but annoying tick found on dogs.

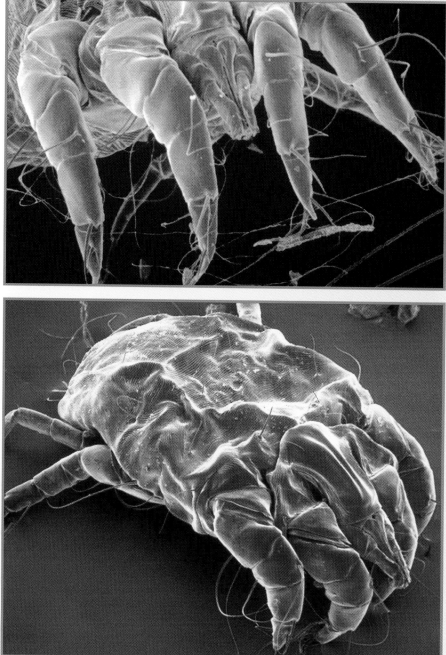

Two views of the mange mite, *Psoroptes bovis.*

SEM BY JAMES HAYDEN-YOAV/PHOTOTAKE

SEM BY JAMES HAYDEN-YOAV/PHOTOTAKE

INTERNAL PARASITES

Most animals—fishes, birds and mammals, including dogs and humans—have worms and other parasites that live inside their bodies. According to Dr Herbert R Axelrod, the fish pathologist, there are two kinds of parasites: dumb and smart. The smart parasites live in peaceful cooperation with their hosts (symbiosis), while the dumb parasites kill their host. Most of the worm infections are relatively easy to control. If they are not controlled they eventually weaken the host dog to the point that other medical problems occur, but they are not dumb parasites.

ROUNDWORMS

The roundworms that infect dogs are scientifically known as *Toxocara canis*. They live in the dog's intestine. The worms shed eggs continually. It has been estimated that a dog produces about 150 grammes of faeces every day. Each gramme of faeces averages 10,000–12,000 eggs of roundworms. There are no known areas in which dogs roam that do not contain roundworm eggs. The greatest danger of roundworms

Did You Know?

Ridding your puppy of worms is VERY IMPORTANT because certain worms that puppies carry, such as tapeworms and roundworms, can infect humans.

Breeders initiate a deworming programme at or about four weeks of age. The routine is repeated every two or three weeks until the puppy is three months old. The breeder from whom you obtained your puppy should provide you with the complete details of the deworming programme.

Your veterinary surgeon can prescribe and monitor the programme of deworming for you. The usual programme is treating the puppy every 15–20 days until the puppy is positively worm free.

It is not advised that you treat your puppy with drugs that are not recommended professionally.

PHOTO BY CAROLINA BIOLOGICAL SUPPLY/PHOTOTAKE.

The roundworm, *Rhabditis.* The roundworm can infect both dogs and humans.

The roundworm *Rhabditis*.

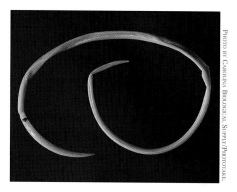

PHOTO BY CAROLINA BIOLOGICAL SUPPLY/PHOTOTAKE.

PHOTO BY DWIGHT R KUHN.

Male and female hookworms, *Ancylostoma caninum*, are uncommonly found in pet or show dogs in Britain. Hookworms may infect other dogs that have exposure to grasslands.

is that they infect people, too! It is wise to have your dog tested regularly for roundworms.

Pigs also have roundworm infections that can be passed to human and dogs. The typical roundworm parasite is called *Ascaris lumbricoides*.

HOOKWORMS

The worm *Ancylostoma caninum* is commonly called the dog hookworm. It is dangerous to humans and cats. It also has teeth by which

it attaches itself to the intestines of the dog. It changes the site of its attachment about six times a day and the dog loses blood from each detachment, possibly causing iron-deficiency anaemia. Hookworms are easily purged from the dog with many medications. Milbemycin oxime, which also serves as a heartworm preventative in Collies, can be used for this purpose.

In Britain the 'temperate climate' hookworm (*Uncinaria stenocephala*) is rarely found in pet or show dogs, but can occur in hunting packs, racing Greyhounds and sheepdogs because the worms can be prevalent wherever dogs are exercised regularly on grassland.

Did You Know?

Caring for the puppy starts before the puppy is born by keeping the dam healthy and well-nourished. Most puppies have worms, even if they are not evident, so a worming programme is essential. The worms continually shed eggs except during their dormant stage, when they just rest in the tissues of the puppy. During this stage they are not evident during a routine examination.

Did You Know?

Average size dogs can pass 1,360,000 roundworm eggs every day.

For example, if there were only 1 million dogs in the world, the world would be saturated with 1,300 metric tonnes of dog faeces.

These faeces would contain 15,000,000,000 roundworm eggs.

7–31% of home gardens and children's play boxes in the U. S. contain roundworm eggs.

Flushing dog's faeces down the toilet is not a safe practice because the usual sewage treatments do not destroy roundworm eggs.

Infected puppies start shedding roundworm eggs at 3 weeks of age. They can be infected by their mother's milk.

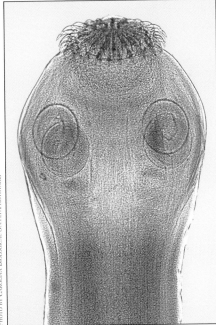

The infective stage of the hookworm larva.

PHOTO BY C JAMES WEBB/PHOTOTAKE.

The head and rostellum (the round prominence on the scolex) of a tapeworm, which infects dogs and humans.

PHOTO BY CAROLINA BIOLOGICAL SUPPLY/PHOTOTAKE.

TAPEWORMS

There are many species of tapeworms. They are carried by fleas! The dog eats the flea and starts the tapeworm cycle. Humans can also be infected with tapeworms, so don't eat fleas! Fleas are so small that your dog could pass them onto your hands, your plate or your food and thus make it possible for you to ingest a flea which is carrying tapeworm eggs.

While tapeworm infection is not life threatening in dogs (smart parasite!), it can be the cause of a very serious liver disease for humans. About 50 percent of the humans infected with *Echinococ-*

cus multilocularis, a type of tapeworm that causes alveolar hydatis, perish.

HEARTWORMS

Heartworms are thin, extended worms up to 30 cms (12 ins) long which live in a dog's heart and the major blood vessels surrounding it. Dogs may have up to 200 of these worms. The symptoms may be loss of energy, loss of appetite, coughing, the development of a pot belly and anaemia.

Heartworms are transmitted by mosquitoes. The mosquito drinks the blood of an infected dog and takes in larvae with the blood. The larvae, called microfilaria, develop within the body of the mosquito and are passed on to the next dog bitten after the larvae mature. It takes two to three weeks for the larvae to develop to the infective stage within the body of the mosquito. Dogs should be treated at about six weeks of age, then every six months.

Blood testing for heartworms is not necessarily indicative of

Did You Know?

Humans, rats, squirrels, foxes, coyotes, wolves, mixed breeds of dogs and purebred dogs are all susceptible to tapeworm infection. Except in humans, tapeworms are usually not a fatal infection.

Infected individuals can harbour a thousand parasitic worms.

Tapeworms have two sexes—male and female (many other worms have only one sex—male and female in the same worm).

If dogs eat infected rats or mice, they get the tapeworm disease.

One month after attaching to a dog's intestine, the worm starts shedding eggs. These eggs are infective immediately.

Infective eggs can live for a few months without a host animal.

Roundworms, whipworms and tapeworms are just a few of the other commonly known worms that infect dogs.

how seriously your dog is infected. This is a dangerous disease. Although heartworm is a problem for dogs in America, Australia, Asia and Central Europe, dogs in the United Kingdom are not affected by heartworm.

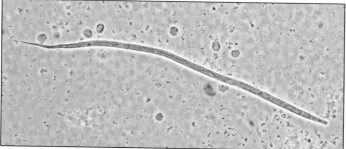

The heartworm, *Dirofilaria immitis*.

PHOTO BY JAMES E HAYDEN, RPB/PHOTOTAKE

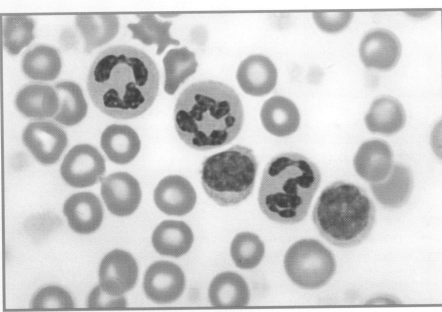

Magnified
heartworm
larvae,
*Dirofilaria
immitis.*

The heart
of a dog infected
with canine heart-
worm, *Dirofilaria
immitis.*

127

BREED-SPECIFIC MEDICAL CONCERNS

Though Shetland Sheepdogs are hardy, long-lived dogs, the breed is subject to certain health conditions. It behooves the potential puppy buyer to be aware of these problems and avoid them wherever possible.

Because of the Sheltie's heavy coat, skin problems can arise if coat care is neglected. They need to be brushed daily to remove foreign matter and dead hair, which if left in the coat, will cause matting. They don't need grooming by a professional groomer, but they must be brushed daily and bathed when necessary.

Eye problems such as PRA (progressive retinal atrophy), cataracts, ectasia syndrome and trichiasis are all seen in the breed. Have the puppy examined and tested by a veterinary ophthalmol-

ogist as early as eight to ten weeks of age to determine if the puppy is a candidate for these problems.

Hip dysplasia, epilepsy, thyroid deficiency, Collie nose (nasal dermatitis), deafness (particularly in blue merles) and von Willebrand's disease (blood-clotting disease) are well documented in the breed. When you see a litter of Sheltie puppies, ask the breeder about these and any other health problems that the parents may have. Some of these problems are genetic and can be passed on to the puppy you buy. Today there are certain tests that can be used to certify that the parents are free from the genes that cause them in the dogs and/or their offspring. Regardless of how appealing a puppy is to a buyer, possessing the potential to have one of these problems makes 'cute' totally irrelevent.

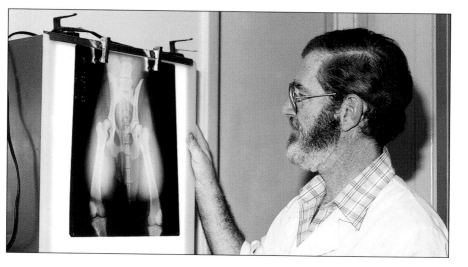

Broken bones, hip and elbow dysplasia and other maladies are often readily discernible with radiographic examination.

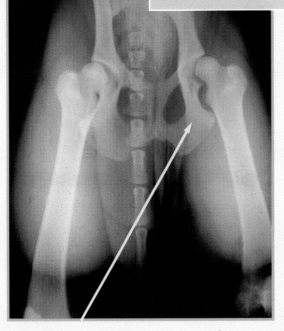

DO YOU KNOW ABOUT HIP DYSPLASIA?

Hip dysplasia is a fairly common condition found in purebred dogs. When a dog has hip dysplasia, its hind leg has an incorrectly formed hip joint. By constant use of the hip joint, it becomes more and more loose, wears abnormally and may become arthritic.

Hip dysplasia can only be confirmed with an X-ray, but certain symptoms may indicate a problem. Your dog may have a hip dysplasia problem if it walks in a peculiar manner, hops instead of smoothly runs, uses his hind legs in unison (to keep the pressure off the weak joint), has trouble getting up from a prone position or always sits with both legs together on one side of its body.

As the dog matures, it may adapt well to life with a bad hip, but in a few years the arthritis develops and many dogs with hip dysplasia become cripples.

Hip dysplasia is considered an inherited disease and can usually be diagnosed when the dog is three to nine months old. Some experts claim that a special diet might help your puppy outgrow the bad hip, but the usual treatments are surgical. The removal of the pectineus muscle, the removal of the round part of the femur, reconstructing the pelvis and replacing the hip with an artificial one are all surgical interventions that are expensive, but they are usually very successful. Follow the advice of your veterinary surgeon.

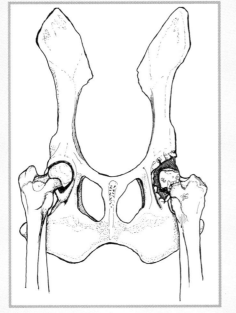

Hip dysplasia is a badly worn hip joint caused by improper fit of the bone into the socket. It is easily the most common hip problem in larger dogs. The illustration shows a healthy hip joint on the left and an unhealthy hip joint on the right.

The term old is a qualitative term. For dogs, as well as their masters, old is relative. Certainly we can all distinguish between a puppy Shetland Sheepdog and an adult Shetland Sheepdog—there are the obvious physical traits, such as size, appearance and facial expressions, and personality traits. Puppies that are nasty are very rare. Puppies and young dogs like to play with children. Children's natural exuberance is a good match for the seemingly endless energy of young dogs. They like to run, jump, chase and retrieve. When dogs grow up and cease their interaction with children, they are often thought of as being too old to play with the kids.

On the other hand, if a Shetland Sheepdog is only exposed to people over 60 years of age, its life will normally be less active and it will not seem to be getting old as its activity level slows down.

Growing old happens to dogs just as it does to people. And as with people, ageing includes such manifestations as confusion, memory lapses, physical deterioration, pain, serious illnesses and even personality changes. The large breeds are usually considered seniors by 10 to 12 years of age. Smaller breeds often do not show signs of ageing until they are 14 to 16 years old. Shelties follow this smaller dog tendency by living well into their mid-teens.

WHAT TO LOOK FOR IN SENIORS
Most veterinary surgeons and behaviourists use the seventh year mark as the time to consider a dog a 'senior.' The term 'senior' does not imply that the dog is geriatric and has begun to fail in mind and body. Ageing is essentially a slowing process. Humans readily admit that they feel a difference in

Did You Know?
The bottom line is simply that a dog is getting old when YOU think it is getting old because it slows down in its general activities, including walking, running, eating, jumping and retrieving. On the other hand, certain activities increase, such as more sleeping, more barking and more repetition of habits like going to the door without being called when you put your coat on to leave or go outdoors.

CDS: COGNITIVE DYSFUNCTION SYNDROME
'Old Dog Syndrome'

There are many ways for you to evaluate old-dog syndrome. Veterinary surgeons have defined CDS (cognitive dysfunction syndrome) as the gradual deterioration of cognitive abilities. These are indicated by changes in the dog's behaviour. When a dog changes its routine response, and maladies have been eliminated as the cause of these behavioural changes, then CDS is the usual diagnosis.

More than half the dogs over 8 years old suffer some form of CDS. The older the dog, the more chance it has of suffering from CDS. In humans, doctors often dismiss the CDS behavioural changes as part of 'winding down.'

There are four major signs of CDS: frequent toilet accidents inside the home, sleeps much more or much less than normal, acts confused, and fails to respond to social stimuli.

SYMPTOMS OF CDS

FREQUENT TOILET ACCIDENTS
- *Urinates in the house.*
- *Defecates in the house.*
- *Doesn't signal that he wants to go out.*

SLEEP PATTERNS
- *Moves much more slowly.*
- *Sleeps more than normal during the day.*
- *Sleeps less during the night.*
- *Walks around listlessly and without a destination goal.*

CONFUSION
- *Goes outside and just stands there.*
- *Appears confused with a faraway look in his eyes.*
- *Hides more often.*
- *Doesn't recognise friends.*
- *Doesn't come when called.*

FAILS TO RESPOND TO SOCIAL STIMULI
- *Comes to people less frequently, whether called or not.*
- *Doesn't tolerate petting for more than a short time.*
- *Doesn't come to the door when you return home from work.*

As your Sheltie enters his golden years, he deserves all the comforts of home. It may be time to surrender a cosy spot on the couch to your old friend.

their activity level from age 20 to 30, and then from 30 to 40, etc. By treating the seven-year-old dog as a senior, owners are able to implement certain therapeutic and preventive medical strategies with the help of their veterinary surgeons. A senior-care programme should include at least two veterinary visits per year, screening sessions to determine the dog's health status, as well as nutritional counselling. Veterinary surgeons determine the senior dog's health status through a blood smear for a complete blood count, serum chemistry profile with electrolytes, urinalysis, blood pressure check, electrocardiogram, ocular tonometry (pressure on the eyeball), and dental prophylaxis.

Such an extensive programme for senior dogs is well advised before owners start to see the obvious physical signs of ageing, such as slower and inhibited movement, greying, increased sleep/nap periods, and disinterest in play and other activity. This preventative programme promises a longer, healthier life for the ageing dog. Amongst the physical problems common in ageing dogs are the loss of sight and hearing, arthritis, kidney and liver failure, diabetes mellitus, heart disease and Cushing's disease (a hormonal disease).

In addition to the physical manifestations discussed, there

When Your Dog Gets Old...
Signs the Owner Can Look For

IF YOU NOTICE...	IT COULD INDICATE...
Discolouration of teeth and gums, foul breath, loss of appetite	Abcesses, gum disease, mouth lesions
Lumps, bumps, cysts, warts, fatty tumours	Cancers, benign or malignant
Cloudiness of eyes, apparent loss of sight.	Cataracts, lenticular sclerosis, PRA, retinal dysplasia, blindness
Flaky coat, alopaecia (hair loss)	Hormonal problems, hypothyroidism
Obesity, appetite loss, excessive weight gain	Various problems
Household accidents, increased urination	Diabetes, kidney or bladder disease
Increased thirst	Kidney disease, diabetes mellitus
Change in sleeping habits, coughing	Heart disease
Difficulty moving	Arthritis, degenerative joint disease, spondylosis (degenerative spine disease)

If you notice any of these signs, an appointment should be made immediately with a veterinary surgeon for a thorough evaluation.

DID YOU KNOW?
Your senior dog may lose interest in eating, not because he's less hungry but because his senses of smell and taste have diminished.
The old chow simply does not smell as good as it once did. Additionally, older dogs use less energy and thereby can sustain themselves on less food.

are some behavioural changes and problems related to ageing dogs. Dogs suffering from hearing or vision loss, dental discomfort or arthritis can become aggressive. Likewise the near-deaf and/or blind dog may be startled more easily and react in an unexpectedly aggressive manner. Seniors suffering from senility can become more impatient and irritable. Housesoiling accidents are associated with loss of mobility, kidney problems and loss of sphincter control as well as plaque accumulation, physiological brain changes and reactions to medications. Older dogs, just like young puppies, suffer from separation anxiety, which can lead to excessive barking, whining, housesoiling and destructive behaviour. Seniors may become fearful of everyday sounds, such as vacuum cleaners, heaters, thunder and passing traffic. Some dogs have difficulty sleeping, due to discomfort, the need for frequent potty visits and the like.

Owners should avoid spoiling the older dog with too many fatty treats. Obesity is a common problem in older dogs and subtracts years from their lifespan. Keep the senior dog as trim as possible since excessive weight puts additional stress on the body's vital organs. Some breeders recommend supplementing the diet with foods high in fibre and lower in calories. Adding fresh vegetables and marrow broth to the senior's diet makes a tasty, low-calorie, low-fat supplement. Vets also offer specialty diets for senior dogs that are worth exploring.

Your dog, as he nears his twilight years, needs his owner's patience and good care more than ever. Never punish an older dog for an accident or abnormal behaviour. For all the years of love, protection and companionship that your dog has provided, he deserves special attention and

Did You Know?

The symptoms listed below are symptoms that gradually appear and become more noticeable. They are not life threatening; however, the symptoms below are to be taken very seriously and a discussion with your veterinary surgeon is warranted:

• Your dog cries and whimpers when it moves and stops running completely.

• Convulsions start or become more serious and frequent. The usual convulsion (spasm) is when the dog stiffens and starts to tremble being unable or unwilling to move. The seizure usually lasts for 5 to 30 minutes.

• Your dog drinks more water and urinates more frequently. Wetting and bowel accidents take place indoors without warning.

• Vomiting becomes more and more frequent.

courtesies. The older dog may need to relieve himself at 3 a.m. because he can no longer hold it for eight hours. Older dogs may not be able to remain crated for more than two or three hours. It may be time to give up a sofa or chair to your old friend. Although he may not seem as enthusiastic about your attention and petting, he does appreciate the considerations you offer as he gets older.

Your Shetland Sheepdog does not understand why his world is slowing down. Owners must make the transition into the golden years as pleasant and rewarding as possible.

WHAT TO DO WHEN THE TIME COMES

You are never fully prepared to make a rational decision about putting your dog to sleep. It is very obvious that you love your Shetland Sheepdog or you would not be reading this book. Putting a loved dog to sleep is extremely difficult. It is a decision that must be made with your veterinary sur-

geon. You are usually forced to make the decision when one of the life-threatening symptoms listed above becomes serious enough for you to seek medical (veterinary) help.

If the prognosis of the malady indicates the end is near and your beloved pet will only suffer more and experience no enjoyment for the balance of its life, then euthanasia is the right choice.

WHAT IS EUTHANASIA?

Euthanasia derives from the Greek meaning *good death*. In other words, it means the planned, painless killing of a dog suffering from a painful, incurable condition, or who is so aged that it cannot walk, see, eat or control its excretory functions.

Euthanasia is usually accomplished by injection with an overdose of an anaesthesia or barbiturate. Aside from the prick of the needle, the experience is usually painless.

HOW ABOUT YOU?

The decision to euthanize your dog is never easy. The days during which the dog becomes ill and the end occurs can be unusually stressful for you. If this is your first experience with the death of a loved one, you may need the comfort dictated by your religious beliefs. If you are the head of the family and have children, you should have involved them in the decision of putting your Shetland Sheepdog to sleep. Usually your dog can be maintained on drugs for a few days in order to give you ample time to make a decision. During this time, talking with members of your family or even people who have lived through this same experience can ease the burden of your inevitable decision.

THE FINAL RESTING PLACE

Dogs can have some of the same privileges as humans. They can occasionally be buried in a pet cemetery, which is generally expensive, or if they have died at home can be buried in your garden in a place suitably marked with some stone or newly planted tree or bush. Alternatively they can be cremated and the ashes returned to you, or some people prefer to leave their dogs at the surgery for the vet to dispose of.

All of these options should be discussed frankly and openly with your veterinary surgeon. Do not be afraid to ask financial ques-

If you are interested in burying your dog, there are pet cemeteries catering to pet lovers.

Special gravestones and markers often indicate pets' graves; some graves may even be decorated with flowers or favourite toys.

tions. Cremations can be individual, but a less expensive option is mass cremation, although of course the ashes can not then be returned. Vets can usually arrange cremation services on your behalf, but you must be aware that in Britain if your dog has died at the surgery the vet cannot legally allow you to take your dog's body home.

GETTING ANOTHER DOG?

The grief of losing your beloved dog will be as lasting as the grief of losing a human friend or relative. You cannot go out and buy another grandfather, but you can go out and buy another Shetland Sheepdog. In most cases, if your dog died of old age (if there is such a thing), it had slowed down considerably. Do you want a new Shetland Sheepdog puppy to replace it? Or are you better off in finding a more mature Shetland Sheepdog, say two to three years of age, which will usually be housetrained and will have an already developed personality. In this case, you can find out if you like each other after a few hours

of being together.

The decision is, of course, your own. Do you want another Shetland Sheepdog or perhaps a different breed so as to avoid comparison with your beloved friend? Most people usually buy the same breed because they know (and love) the characteristics of that breed. Then, too, they often know people who have the same breed and perhaps they are lucky enough that one of their friends expects a litter soon. What could be better?

Cemeteries for pets usually have a place for funeral urns that will contain your pet's ashes.

137

Showing Your
SHETLAND SHEEPDOG

When you purchased your Shetland Sheepdog you should have made it clear to the breeder whether you wanted one just as a loveable companion and pet, or if you hoped to be buying a Shetland Sheepdog with show prospects. No reputable breeder will sell you a young puppy saying that it was definitely of show quality for so much can go wrong during the early weeks and months of a puppy's development. If you plan to show, what you will hopefully have acquired is a puppy with 'show potential.'

To the novice, exhibiting a Shetland Sheepdog in the show ring may look easy but it usually takes a lot of hard work and devotion to do top winning at a show such as the prestigious Crufts, not to mention a little luck too!

The first concept that the canine novice learns when watching a dog show is that each breed first competes against members of its own breed. Once the judge has selected the best member of each breed, provided that the show is judged on a Group system, that chosen dog will compete with other dogs in its group. Finally the best of each group will compete for Best in Show and Reserve Best in Show.

The second concept that you must understand is that the dogs are not actually compared to one another. The judge compares each dog against the breed standard, which is a written description of the ideal specimen of the breed. Whilst some early breed standards were indeed based on specific dogs that were famous or pop-

This is a very successful Junior Handler who has won many awards with her Shetland Sheepdog. More and more young people are becoming active in the dog fancy.

ular, many dedicated enthusiasts say that a perfect specimen, described in the standard, has never been bred. Thus the 'perfect' dog never walked into a show ring, has never been bred and, to the woe of dog breeders around the globe, does not exist. Breeders attempt to get as close to this ideal as possible, with every litter, but theoretically the 'perfect' dog is so elusive that it is impossible. (And if the 'perfect' dog were born, breeders and judges would never agree that it was indeed 'perfect.')

If you are interested in exploring dog shows, your best bet is to join your local breed club. These clubs often host both Championship and Open shows, and sometimes Match meetings and Special Events, all of which could be of interest, even if you are only an onlooker. Clubs also send out newsletters and some organise training days and seminars in order that people may learn more about their chosen breed. To locate the nearest breed club for you, contact The Kennel Club, the ruling body for the British dog world. The Kennel Club governs not only conformation shows but also working trials, obedience trials, agility trials and field trials. The Kennel Club furnishes the rules and regulations for all these events plus general dog registration and other basic requirements of dog ownership. Its annual show

called the Crufts Dogs Show, held in Birmingham, is the largest bench show in England. Every year around 20,000 of the U.K.'s best dogs qualify to participate in this marvellous show which lasts four days.

The Kennel Club governs many different kinds of shows in Great Britain, Australia, South Africa and beyond. At the most competitive and prestigious of these shows, the Championship Shows, a dog can earn Challenge Certificates, and thereby become a Show Champion or a Champion. A dog must earn three Challenge Certificates under three different judges to earn the prefix of 'Sh Ch' or 'Ch.' Note that some breeds must also qualify in a field trial in order to gain the title of full champion. Challenge Certificates

A well-trained Shetland Sheepdog will perform in the ring for even the youngest handler. Children have much to learn by participating in dog shows.

139

If you are interested in dog shows, you can get valuable information and experience by visiting a local dog show or breed match. Breed clubs host shows especially for their breed.

are awarded to a very small percentage of the dogs competing, especially as dogs which are already Champions compete with others for these coveted CCs. The number of Challenge Certificates awarded in any one year is based upon the total number of dogs in each breed entered for competition. There are three types of Championship Shows, an all-breed General Championship show for all Kennel-Club-recognised breeds; a Group Championship Show, limited to breeds within one of the Groups; and a Breed Show, usually confined to a single breed. The Kennel Club determines which breeds at which Championship Shows will have

the opportunity to earn Challenge Certificates (or tickets). Serious exhibitors often will opt not to participate if the tickets are withheld at a particular show. This policy makes earning championships ever more difficult to accomplish.

Open Shows are generally less competitive and are frequently used as 'practice shows' for young dogs. There are hundreds of Open Shows each year that can be invitingly social events and are great first show experiences for the novice. Even if you're considering just watching a show to wet your paws, an Open Show is a great choice.

Whilst Championship and

Did You Know?

You can get information about dog shows from kennel clubs and breed clubs:

Fédération Cynologique Internationale
14, rue Leopold II, B-6530 Thuin, Belgium
www.fci.be

The Kennel Club
1-5 Clarges St., Piccadilly, London W1Y 8AB, UK
www.the-kennel-club.org.uk

American Kennel Club
5580 Centerview Dr., Raleigh, NC 27606-3390, USA
www.akc.org

Canadian Kennel Club
89 Skyway Ave., Suite 100, Etobicoke, Ontario
M9W 6R4 Canada
www.ckc.ca

Open Shows are most important for the beginner to understand, there are other types of shows in which the interested dog owner can participate. Training clubs sponsor Matches that can be entered on the day of the show for a nominal fee. In these introductory-level exhibitions, two dogs are pulled out of a hat and 'matched,' the winner of that match goes on to the next round, and eventually only one dog is left undefeated.

Exemption Shows are much more light-hearted affairs with usually only four pedigree classes and several 'fun' classes, all of which can be entered on the day. The proceeds of an Exemption Show must be given to a charity and are sometimes held in conjunction with small agricultural shows. Limited Shows are also available in small number, but entry is restricted to members of the club which hosts the show, although one can usually join the club when making an entry.

Before you actually step into the ring, you would be well advised to sit back and observe the judge's ring procedure. If it is your first time in the ring, do not be over-anxious and run to the front of the line. It is much better to stand back and study how the exhibitor in front of you is performing. The judge asks each handler to 'stand' the dog, hopefully showing the dog off to his best advantage. The judge will observe the dog from a distance and from

Winning the Ticket

Earning a championship at Kennel Club shows is the most difficult in the world. Compared to the United States and Canada where it is relatively not 'challenging,' collecting three green tickets not only requires much time and effort, it can be very expensive! Challenge Certificates, as the tickets are properly known, are the building blocks of champions—good breeding, good handling, good training and good luck!

different angles, approach the dog, check his teeth, overall structure, alertness and muscle tone, as well as consider how well the dog 'conforms' to the standard. Most importantly, the judge will have the exhibitor move the dog around the ring in some pattern that he or she should specify (another advantage to not going first, but always listen since some judges change their directions, and the judge is always right!) Finally the judge will give the dog one last look before moving on to the next exhibitor.

If you are not in the top three at your first show, do not be dis-

couraged. Be patient and consistent and you may eventually find yourself in the winning lineup. Remember that the winners were once in your shoes and have devoted many hours and much money to earn the placement. If you find that your dog is losing every time and never getting a nod, it may be time to consider a different dog sport or just enjoy your Shetland Sheepdog as a pet.

Show Ring Etiquette

Just like with anything else, there is a certain etiquette to the show ring that can only be learned through experience. Showing your dog can be quite intimidating to you as a novice when it seems as if everyone else knows what they are doing. You can familiarise yourself with ring procedure beforehand by taking a class to prepare you and your dog for conformation showing or by talking with an experienced handler. When you are in the ring, listen and pay attention to the judge and follow his/her directions. Remember, even the most skilled handlers had to start somewhere. Keep it up and you too will become a proficient handler before too long!

WORKING TRIALS
Working trials can be entered by any well-trained dog of any breed, not just Gundogs or Working dogs. Many dogs that earn the Kennel Club Good Citizen Dog award choose to participate in a working trial. There are five stakes at both open and championship levels: Companion Dog (CD), Utility Dog

basic hurdle with a removable top bar; and a long jump across angled planks.

To earn the UD, WD and TD, dogs must track approximately one-half mile for articles laid from one-half hour to three hours ago. Tracks consist of turns and legs, and fresh ground is used for each participant.

The fifth stake, PD, involves teaching manwork, which is not recommended for every breed.

FIELD TRIALS AND WORKING TESTS

Working tests are frequently used to prepare dogs for field trials, the purpose of which is to heighten

(UD), Working Dog (WD), Tracking Dog (TD) and Patrol Dog (PD). As in conformation shows, dogs compete against a standard and if the dog reaches the qualifying mark, it obtains a certificate. Divided into groups, each exercise must be achieved 70 percent in order to qualify. If the dog achieves 80 percent in the open level, it receives a Certificate of Merit (COM), in the championship level, it receives a Qualifying Certificate. At the CD stake, dogs must participate in four groups, Control, Stay, Agility and Search (Retrieve and Nosework). At the next three levels, UD, WD and TD, there are only three groups: Control, Agility and Nosework.

Agility consists of three jumps: a vertical scale up a wall of planks; a clear jump over a

Classes at Dog Shows

There can be as many as 18 classes per sex for your breed. Check the show schedule carefully to make sure that you have entered your dog in the appropriate class. Among the classes offered can be: Beginners; Minor Puppy (ages 6 to 9 months); Puppy (ages 6 to 12 months); Junior (ages 6 to 18 months); Beginners (handler or dog never won first place) as well as the following, each of which is defined in the schedule: Maiden; Novice; Tyro; Debutant; Undergraduate; Graduate; Postgraduate; Minor Limit; Mid Limit; Limit; Open; Veteran; Stud Dog; Brood Bitch; Progeny; Brace and Team.

Trainable, athletic and ever-ready for a challenge, Shelties regularly perform and excel in agility trials. They easily handle the collapsible tunnel (above) and the bar jumps (below).

the instincts and natural abilities of gundogs. Live game is not used in working tests. Unlike field trials, working tests do not count toward a dog's record at The Kennel Club, though the same judges often oversee working tests. Field trials began in England in 1947 and are only moderately popular amongst dog folk. Whilst breeders of Working and Gundog breeds concern themselves with the field abilities of their dogs, there is considerably less interest in field trials than dog shows. In order for dogs to become full champions, certain breeds must qualify in the field as well. Upon gaining three CCs in the show ring, the dog is designated a Show Champion (Sh Ch). The title Champion (Ch) requires that the dog gain an award at a field trial, be a 'special qualifier' at a field trial or pass a 'special show dog qualifier' judged by a field trial judge on a shooting day.

AGILITY TRIALS
Agility trials began in the United Kingdom in 1977 and have since spread around the world, especially to the United States, where it enjoys strong popularity. The handler directs his dog over an obstacle course that includes jumps (such as those used in the working trials), as well as tyres, the dog walk, weave poles, pipe tunnels, collapsed tunnels, etc. The Kennel Club requires that

dogs not be trained for agility until they are 12 months old. This dog sport intends to be great fun for dog and owner and interested owners should join a training club that has obstacles and experienced agility handlers who can introduce you and your dog to the 'ropes' (and tyres, tunnels and so on).

FÉDÉRATION CYNOLOGIQUE INTERNATIONALE

Established in 1911, the Fédération Cynologique Internationale (FCI) represents the 'world kennel club.' This international body brings uniformity to the breeding, judging and showing of purebred dogs. Although the FCI originally included only four European nations: France, Holland, Austria and Belgium (which remains its headquarters), the organisation

FCI Breeds

There are 329 breeds recognised by the FCI, and each breed is considered to be 'owned' by a specific country. Each breed standard is a cooperative effort between the breed's country and the FCI's Standards and Scientific Commissions. Judges use these official breed standards at shows held in FCI member countries. One of the functions of the FCI is to update and translate the breed standards into French, English, Spanish and German.

Shelties demonstrating their skill at an agility trial on the tyre jump (above) and the weave poles (below).

145

today embraces nations on six continents and recognises well over 300 breeds of purebred dog. There are three titles attainable through the FCI: the International Champion, which is the most prestigious; the International Beauty Champion, which is based on aptitude certificates in different countries; and the International Trial Champion, which is based on achievement in obedience trials in different countries. Quarantine laws in England and Australia prohibit most of their exhibitors from entering FCI shows. The rest of the Continent does participate in these impressive canine spectacles, the largest of which is the World Dog Show, hosted in a different country each year. FCI sponsors both national and international shows. The

Did You Know?

The Kennel Club divides its dogs into seven Groups: Gundogs, Utility, Working, Toy, Terrier, Hounds and Pastoral.*

*The Pastoral Group, established in 1999, includes those sheepdog breeds previously categorised in the Working Group.

hosting country determines the judging system and breed standards are always based on the breed's country of origin.

The FCI is divided into ten 'Groups.' At the World Dog Show, the following 'Classes' are offered for each breed: Puppy Class (6–9 months), Youth Class (9–18 months), Open Class (15 months or older) and Champion Class. A dog can be awarded a classification of Excellent, Very Good, Good, Sufficient and Not Sufficient. Puppies can be awarded classifications of Very Promising, Promising or Not Promising. Four placements are made in each class. After all sexes and classes are judged, a Best of Breed is selected. Other special groups and classes may also be shown. Each exhibitor showing a dog receives a written evaluation from the judge.

Besides the World Dog Show, you can exhibit your dog at speciality shows held by different breed clubs. Speciality shows may have their own regulations.

Did You Know?

The FCI *does not* issue pedigrees. The FCI members and contract partners are responsible for issuing pedigrees and training judges in their own countries. The FCI does maintain a list of judges and makes sure that they are recognised throughout the FCI member countries.

The FCI also *does not* act as a breeder referral; breeder information is available from FCI-recognised national canine societies in each of the FCI's member countries.

Understanding the Behaviour of Your SHETLAND SHEEPDOG

As a Shetland Sheepdog owner, you have selected your dog so that you and your loved ones can have a companion, a protector, a friend and a four-legged family member. You invest time, money and effort to care for and train the family's new charge. Of course, this chosen canine behaves perfectly! Well, perfectly like a dog.

THINK LIKE A DOG

Dogs do not think like humans, nor do humans think like dogs, though we try. Unfortunately, a dog is incapable of figuring out how humans think, so the responsibility falls on the owner to adopt a proper canine mindset. Dogs cannot rationalise, and dogs exist in the present moment. Many dog owners make the mistake in training of thinking that they can reprimand their dog for something he did a while ago. Basically, you cannot even reprimand a dog for something he did 20 seconds ago! Either catch him in the act or forget it! It is a waste of your and your dog's time—in his mind, you are reprimanding him for whatever he is doing at that moment.

The following behavioural problems represent some which owners most commonly encounter. Every dog is unique and every situation is unique. No author could purport to solve your Shetland Sheepdog's problem simply by reading a script. Here we outline some basic 'dogspeak' so that owners' chances of solving behavioural problems are increased. Discuss bad habits with your veterinary surgeon and he/she can recommend a behavioural specialist to consult in appropriate cases. Since behavioural abnormalities are the leading reason owners abandon their pets, we hope that you will make a valiant effort to solve your Shetland Sheepdog's problem. Patience and understanding are virtues that dwell in every pet-loving household.

Did You Know?

Your dog inherited the pack-leader mentality. He only knows about pecking order. He instinctively wants to be top dog, but you have to convince him that you are boss. There is no such thing as living in a democracy with your dog—you are the one who sets the rules.

SEXUAL BEHAVIOUR

Dogs exhibit certain sexual behaviours that may have influenced your choice of male or female when you first purchased your Shetland Sheepdog. To a certain extent, spaying/neutering will eliminate these behaviours, but if you are purchasing a dog that you wish to breed, you should be aware of what you will have to deal with throughout the dog's life.

Female dogs usually have two oestruses per year with each season lasting about three weeks.

Did You Know?

Males, whether castrated or not, will mount almost anything: a pillow, your leg or, much to your horror, even your neighbour's leg. As with other types of inappropriate behaviour, the dog must be corrected while in the act, which for once is not difficult. Often he will not let go! While a puppy is experimenting with his very first urges, his owners feel he needs to 'sow his oats' and allow the pup to mount. As the pup grows into a full-size dog, with full-size urges, it becomes a nuisance and an embarrassment. Males always appear as if they are trying to 'save the race,' more determined and stronger than imaginable. While altering the dog at an appropriate age will limit the dog's desire, it usually does not remove it entirely.

These are the only times in which a female dog will mate, and she usually will not allow this until the second week of the cycle, but this does vary from bitch to bitch. If not bred during the heat cycle, it is not uncommon for a bitch to experience a false pregnancy, in which her mammary glands swell and she exhibits maternal tendencies toward toys or other objects.

Owners must further recognise that mounting is not merely a sexual expression but also one of dominance. Be consistent and persistent and you will find that you can 'move mounters.'

CHEWING

The national canine pastime is chewing! Every dog loves to sink his 'canines' into a tasty bone, but sometimes that bone is attached to his owner's hand! Dogs need to chew, to massage their gums, to make their new teeth feel better and to exercise their jaws. This is a natural behaviour deeply imbedded in all things canine. Our role as owners is not to stop the dog's chewing, but to redirect it to positive, chew-worthy objects. Be an informed owner and purchase proper chew toys like strong nylon bones that will not splinter. Be sure that the devices are safe and durable, since your dog's safety is at risk. Again, the owner is responsible for ensuring a dog-proof environment. The best answer is prevention: that is, put

It is vital to direct a Sheltie puppy's enthusiasm for play and merrymaking before he develops bad habits that are difficult to undo.

your shoes, handbags and other tasty objects in their proper places (out of the reach of the growing canine mouth). Direct puppies to their toys whenever you see them tasting the furniture legs or the leg of your trousers. Make a loud noise to attract the pup's attention and immediately escort him to his chew toy and engage him with the toy for at least four minutes, praising and encouraging him all the while.

Some trainers recommend deterrents, such as hot pepper or another bitter spice, or a product designed for this purpose, to discourage the dog from chewing unwanted objects. Test out these products yourself before investing in a large quantities.

JUMPING UP
Jumping up is a dog's friendly way of saying hello! Some dog owners do not mind when their dog jumps up, which is fine for them. The problem arises when guests come to the house and the dog greets them in the same manner—whether they like it or not! However friendly the greeting may be, the chances are that your visitors will not appreciate your dog's enthusiasm. The dog will not be able to distinguish upon whom he can jump and whom he cannot. Therefore, it is probably best to discourage this behaviour entirely.

Pick a command such as 'Off.' (avoid using 'Down' since you will use that for the dog to lie down) and tell him 'Off' when he jumps up. Place him on the ground on all fours and have him sit, praising him the whole time. Always lavish him with praise and petting when he is in the sit position. That way you are still giving him a warm affectionate greeting, because you are as excited to see him as he is to see you!

DIGGING
Digging, which is seen as a destructive behaviour to humans, is actually quite a natural behaviour in dogs. Although your Sheltie is not one of the 'earth dogs' (also known as terriers), his desire to dig can be irrepressible and most frustrating to his owners. When digging occurs in your garden, it is actually a normal behaviour redirected into some-

thing the dog can do in his every-day life. In the wild, a dog would be actively seeking food, making his own shelter, etc. He would be using his paws in a purposeful manner for his survival. Since you provide him with food and shelter, he has no need to use his paws for these purposes, and so the energy that he would be using may manifest itself in the form of little holes all over your garden and flower beds.

Perhaps your dog is digging as a reaction to boredom—it is somewhat similar to someone eating a whole bag of crisps in front of the TV—because they are there and there is not anything better to do! Basically, the answer is to provide the dog with adequate play and exercise so that his mind and paws are occupied, and so that he feels as if he is doing something useful.

Of course, digging is easiest to control if it is stopped as soon as possible, but it is often hard to

> ## Did You Know?
> Stop a dog from jumping before he jumps. If he is getting ready to jump onto you, simply walk away. If he jumps on you before you can turn away, lift your knee so that it bumps him in the chest. Do not be forceful. Your dog will realise that jumping up is not a productive way of getting attention.

catch a dog in the act. If your dog is a compulsive digger and is not easily distracted by other activities, you can designate an area on your property where it is okay for him to dig. If you catch him digging in an off-limits area of the garden, immediately bring him to the approved area and praise him for digging there. Keep a close eye on him so that you can catch him in the act—that is the only way to make him understand what is permitted and what is not. If you take him to a hole he dug an hour ago and tell him 'No,' he will understand that you are not fond of holes, or dirt, or flowers. If you catch him whilst he is stifle-deep in your tulips, that is when he will get your message.

BARKING
Dogs cannot talk—oh, what they would say if they could! Instead, barking is a dog's way of 'talking.' It can be somewhat frustrating

> ## Did You Know?
> Punishment is rarely necessary for a misbehaving dog. Dogs that are habitually bad probably had a poor education and they do not know what is expected of them. They need training. Disciplinary behaviour on your part usually does more harm than good.

because it is not always easy to tell what a dog means by his bark—is he excited, happy, frightened or angry? Whatever it is that the dog is trying to say, he should not be punished for barking. It is only when the barking becomes excessive, and when the excessive barking becomes a bad habit, that the behaviour needs to be modified. Shetland Sheepdogs are rather vocal dogs, and they tend to use their barks to express many sentiments. This can be limited by discouraging excessive barking in a Sheltie pup through early training.

If an intruder came into your home in the middle of the night and your Shetland Sheepdog barked a warning, wouldn't you be pleased? You would probably deem your dog a hero, a wonderful guardian and protector of the home. However, if a friend drops by unexpectedly and rings the doorbell and is greeted with a sudden sharp bark, you would probably be annoyed at the dog.

But in reality, isn't this just the same behaviour? The dog does not know any better...unless he sees who is at the door and it is someone he knows, he will bark as a means of vocalising that his (and your) territory is being threatened. Whilst your friend is not posing a threat, it is all the same to the dog. Barking is his means of letting you know that there is an intrusion, whether friend or foe, on your property. This type of barking is instinctive and should not be discouraged.

Excessive habitual barking, however, is a problem that should be corrected early on. As your Shetland Sheepdog grows up, you will be able to tell when his barking is purposeful and when it is for no reason. You will become able to distinguish your dog's different barks and their meanings.

For example, the bark when someone comes to the door will be different from the bark when he is excited to see you. It is similar to a person's tone of voice, except that the dog has to rely totally on tone of voice because he does not have the benefit of using words. An incessant barker will be evident at an early age.

There are some things that encourage a dog to bark. For example, if your dog barks nonstop for a few minutes and you give him a treat to quieten him, he believes that you are rewarding him for barking. He will associate barking with getting a treat, and will keep doing it until he is rewarded.

FOOD STEALING

Is your dog devising ways of stealing food from your coffee table? If so, you must answer the following questions: Is your Shetland Sheepdog hungry, or is he 'constantly famished' like many dogs seem to be? Face it, some dogs are more food-motivated than others. Some dogs are totally obsessed by the smell of food and can only think of their next meal. Food stealing is terrific fun and always yields a great reward—FOOD, glorious food.

The owner's goal, therefore, is to be sensible about where food is placed in the home, and to reprimand your dog whenever caught in the act of stealing. But remem-

Begging is an easy behaviour to avoid, but a difficult one to correct. Never give in to a dog that is begging at the table. Once you give in to a dog who begs, you will be living with a beggar for a lifetime.

ber, only reprimand the dog if you actually see him stealing, not later when the crime is discovered for that will be of no use at all and will only serve to confuse.

BEGGING

Just like food stealing, begging is a favourite pastime of hungry puppies! It yields that same lovely reward—FOOD! Dogs quickly learn that their owners keep the 'good food' for themselves, and that we humans do not dine on dried food alone. Begging is a conditioned response related to a specific stimulus, time and place.

The sounds of the kitchen, cans and bottles opening, crinkling bags, the smell of food in preparation, etc., will excite the dog and soon the paws are in the air!

Here is the solution to stopping this behaviour: Never give in to a beggar! You are rewarding the dog for sitting pretty, jumping up, whining and rubbing his nose into you by giving him that glorious reward—food. By ignoring the dog, you will (eventually) force the behaviour into extinction. Note that the behaviour likely gets worse before it disappears, so be sure there are not any 'softies' in the family who will give in to little 'Oliver' every time he whimpers, 'More, please.'

SEPARATION ANXIETY

Your Shetland Sheepdog may howl, whine or otherwise vocalise his displeasure at your leaving the house and his being left alone. This is a normal reaction, no different from the child who cries as his mother leaves him on the first day at school. In fact, constant attention can lead to separation anxiety in the first place. If you are endlessly fussing over your dog, he will come to expect this from you all of the time and it will be more traumatic for him when you are not there. Obviously, you enjoy spending time with your dog, and he thrives on your love and attention. However, it should not become a dependent

> ### Did You Know?
> The number of dogs who suffer from separation anxiety is on the rise as more and more pet owners find themselves at work all day. New attention is being paid to this problem, which is especially hard to diagnose since it is only evident when the dog is alone. Research is currently being done to help educate dog owners about separation anxiety and about how they can help minimise this problem in their dogs.

relationship where he is heartbroken without you.

One thing you can do to minimise separation anxiety is to make your entrances and exits as low-key as possible. Do not give your dog a long drawn-out goodbye, and do not overly lavish him with hugs and kisses when you return. This is giving in to the attention that he craves, and it will only make him miss it more when you are away. Another thing you can try is to give your dog a treat when you leave; this will not only keep him occupied and keep his mind off the fact that you have just left, but it will also help him associate your leaving with a pleasant experience.

You may have to accustom your dog to being left alone in intervals. Of course, when your dog starts whimpering as you approach the door, your first instinct will be to run to him and comfort him, but do not do it! Really—eventually he will adjust and be just fine if you take it in small steps. His anxiety stems from being placed in an unfamiliar situation; by familiarising him with being alone he will learn that he is okay. That is not to say you should purposely leave your dog home alone, but the dog needs to know that whilst he can depend on you for his care, you do not have to be by his side 24 hours a day.

When the dog is alone in the house, he should be confined to his designated dog-proof area of the house. This should be the area in which he sleeps and already feels comfortable so he will feel more at ease when he is alone.

COPROPHAGIA

Faeces eating is, to most humans, one of the most disgusting behaviours that their dog could engage in, yet to the dog it is perfectly normal. It is hard for us to understand why a dog would want to eat its own fae-

Did You Know?

If you are approached by an aggressive, growling dog, do not run away. Simply stand still and avoid eye contact. If you have something in your hand (like a handbag), throw it sideways away from your body to distract the dog from making a frontal attack.

enough food. If changes in his diet do not seem to work, and no medical cause can be found, you will have to modify the behaviour before it becomes a habit through environmental control. The best way to prevent your dog from eating his stool is to make it unavailable—clean up after he eliminates and remove any stool from the garden. If it is not there, he cannot eat it.

ces. He could be seeking certain nutrients that are missing from his diet, he could be just plain hungry or he could be attracted by the pleasing (to a dog) scent. Whilst coprophagia most often refers to the dog eating his own faeces, a dog may just as likely eat that of another animal as well if he comes across it. Vets have found that diets with a low digestibility, containing relatively low levels of fibre and high levels of starch, increase coprophagia. Therefore, high-fibre diets may decrease the likelihood of dogs eating faeces. Both the consistency of the stool (how firm it feels in the dog's mouth) and the presence of undigested nutrients increase the likelihood. Dogs often find the stool of cats and horses more palatable than that of other dogs. Once the dog develops diarrhoea from faeces eating, it will likely quit this distasteful habit.

To discourage this behaviour, first make sure that the food you are feeding your dog is nutritionally complete and that he is getting

Did You Know?

When a dog bites there is always a good reason for it doing so. Many dogs are trained to protect a person, an area or an object. When that person, area or object is violated, the dog will attack. A dog attacks with its mouth. It has no other means of attack. It never uses teeth for defense. It merely runs away or lays down on the ground when it is in an indefensible situation. Fighting dogs (and there are many breeds which fight) are taught to fight, but they also have a natural instinct to fight. This instinct is normally reserved for other dogs, though unfortunate accidents occur when babies crawl towards a fighting dog and the dog mistakes the crawling child as a potential attacker.

If a dog is a biter for no reason, if it bites the hand that feeds it or if it snaps at members of your family, see your veterinary surgeon or behaviourist immediately to learn how to modify the dog's behaviour.

INDEX

*Page numbers in **boldface** indicate illustrations.*

My Shetland Sheepdog

PUT YOUR PUPPY'S FIRST PICTURE HERE

Dog's Name _____

Date _____ Photographer _____